SCHOLASTIC Pocket

Thesaurus

SPECIAL ABRIDGED EDITION

SCHOLASTIC INC.

New York   Toronto   London   Auckland   Sydney   Mexico City
New Delhi   Hong Kong   Buenos Aires

ISBN B-OK9-90827-2

12 11 10 9 8 7 6 5 4 3 2 1   6 7 8 9 10 11/0

Printed in the U.S.A.
First Printing, September 2006

Introduction

Why Use a Thesaurus?

You already know thousands of words. These words are usually all you need. But sometimes, even though you know you have a good idea, you just can't think of quite the right word to express it the way you want. If you start with a word you know, your thesaurus will help you find synonyms to choose from. Synonyms are words that mean the same or nearly the same as other words. Here are some of the ways in which the *Scholastic Pocket Thesaurus* can be helpful:

To avoid repetition. Suppose you have used the same word three or four times in one paragraph or page. Rather than use that word again, you would like to find a different way to express the same idea. Your thesaurus provides you with a variety of synonyms.

To make your meaning clear and precise. When you speak or write, you usually think about what you mean, not about the words you are using. But sometimes the meaning doesn't come out as easily or as clearly as you had hoped. Your thesaurus can help you find words that express your idea more effectively than the words you began with. You may find that looking through the synonyms of a word brings to mind different ways to express your idea. It may even help you understand the idea better yourself.

To avoid overused terms. There are a few words that get used so often in so many different ways that they have run out of energy. They no longer have a sharply defined meaning, even though they give a general impression of what we want to say. It may be easier just to use these words, but they don't say anything specific. Often they lead us into clichés or vague thinking. If you find yourself using such general words as nice or pretty or good, try to pin down your thoughts with synonyms that more specifically describe what you are talking about. Your thesaurus can help you replace those words with synonyms like "delightful," "striking," or "favorable." This will make your writing more energetic and original.

To achieve the proper tone. Sometimes the word you thought of is too informal to be used in a school assignment or for a letter you want to write. You want a more serious word, but can't think of one. Or the opposite may be true. You may be writing a story or poem in a conversational or informal style. When selecting any synonym, you should always take a moment to consider whether it is suitable for the style in which you are writing or speaking.

You already know many of the words in the *Scholastic Pocket Thesaurus*, but you will also find many new words here. Your thesaurus will guide you through this web of words in order to make your writing more clear, more mature, and even more elegant. Most importantly, the *Scholastic Pocket Thesaurus* will help you to write accurately and precisely. In this way, you can communicate your thoughts more easily to others. And that is what you are always trying to do when you speak or write.

How to Use This Book

The *Scholastic Pocket Thesaurus* will help you find synonyms for a word that you have in mind.

Main Entry Words

Synonyms are grouped together after main entry words. These main entries are listed alphabetically and printed in boldface type. Suppose you need a synonym for exaggerate. Your thesaurus has a main entry for exaggerate with nine synonyms:

> **exaggerate** *vb* overstate, overdo, inflate, embellish, embroider, elaborate, gild, magnify, dramatize

If a main entry word has more than one sense or use, the synonyms are grouped in numbered senses, as in the entry for boast, which can be either a verb or a noun:

> **boast** 1. *vb* brag, gloat, crow, show off, vaunt, swagger, exult

2. *n* brag, bragging, vaunt, claim, assertion, bluster, swagger, bravado

Part-of-speech Labels

Each entry or numbered sense has a part-of-speech label that identifies the part of speech of the main entry and the synonyms of each sense. The part-of-speech labels are:

n	noun	*prep*	preposition
vb	verb	*conj*	conjunction
adj	adjective	*interj*	interjection
adv	adverb	*pron*	pronoun

Antonyms

Antonyms are words that mean the opposite of other words. Sometimes you can find a clearer way to express your idea by putting it in opposite terms. Some synonyms are followed by antonyms printed inside parentheses:

afraid *adj* scared, frightened, alarmed, terrified, petrified, aghast, scared, timorous (antonym: brave)

Guide Words

The guide words at the top left and right corners of the pages give the first and last words alphabetically on each page.

An Important Reminder

Teachers have one common complaint about the way thesauruses are used. They complain that often students will pick an unfamiliar synonym without realizing that it does not fit properly into the sentence where they put it. Remember that no two synonyms mean exactly the same thing. Anytime you are not certain whether a synonym is just the one you want, or if you are not sure what it means, look it up in a dictionary. Or ask someone whose judgment and knowledge of the language you can trust.

A

able 1. *adj* capable, competent, qualified, eligible, authorized, suitable, fit
2. *adj* accomplished, proficient, skillful, adept, clever, handy, dexterous, deft, smart, expert, practical

abolish *vb* end, eradicate, exterminate, eliminate, revoke, cancel, obliterate, repeal, rescind, annul, nullify, countermand, disallow, veto, overrule, finish, destroy, erase (antonym: save)

about 1. *adv* approximately, around, roughly, nearly, almost, practically
2. *adv* around, round, all around, everywhere, nearby
3. *prep* concerning, regarding, touching, relating to
4. *prep* around, near, at

absent *adj* away, missing, elsewhere, astray, AWOL, lost (antonym: present)

abuse 1. *vb* misuse, mistreat, torment, oppress, suppress, repress, ill-treat, maltreat, torture, persecute, victimize, molest, harass, hurt, insult, punish
2. *n* misuse, mistreatment, ill-treatment, injury, harm, punishment, torture

accent 1. *n* stress, emphasis, prominence, beat, cadence, diacritic
2. *n* pronunciation, inflection, drawl, twang, burr, dialect
3. *n* decoration

4. *vb* emphasize

accidentally *adv* unintentionally, inadvertently, unwittingly, unconsciously, fortuitously, incidentally (antonym: purposely)

accuracy *n* exactness, precision, correctness, exactitude, truth

act 1. *vb* perform, work, function, operate, execute, stage, carry out, ply, serve, go, do
2. *vb* behave, seem, appear
3. *vb* perform, play, enact, stage, portray, dramatize, impersonate, pose, render, pretend
4. *n* deed, action, feat, accomplishment, achievement, exploit, undertaking, step, work
5. *n* bill, law, decree, statute, ordinance, legislation, rule
6. *n* performance, routine, number, sketch, bit, skit, pretense

active *adj* animated, spirited, dynamic, busy, vibrant, bustling, frenetic, hyperactive, strenuous, athletic, lively, alive (antonym: passive)

add 1. *vb* sum, total, calculate, compute, tally, count, score (antonym: subtract)
2. *vb* combine, include, append, annex, supplement, incorporate, integrate, join

adjacent 1. *adj* adjoining, neighboring, bordering, abutting, tangent, next, next door, near
2. *prep* beside

adjust *vb* alter, modify, regulate, adapt, tailor, accommodate, conform, acclimatize, orient, change, fix, arrange

adopt 1. *vb* embrace, appropriate, assume, espouse, approve, choose, use
2. *vb* foster, take in, raise, rear

advantage *n* benefit, profit, superiority, convenience, vantage, upper hand, asset, virtue, plus, avail

advertise *vb* publicize, announce, promote, proclaim, declare, broadcast, pitch, parade, flaunt, plug, tell, show

advice *n* guidance, counsel, recommendation, suggestion, caution, admonition, tip, warning

affect 1. *vb* influence, impress, move, sway
2. *vb* act, pretend
3. *n* emotion

afraid *adj* scared, frightened, alarmed, terrified, petrified, aghast, timorous, anxious, nervous, cowardly (antonym: brave)

again *adv* once more, anew, afresh, over, encore

agent 1. *n* representative, intermediary, middleman, broker, executor, liaison, delegate, spokesperson, go-between, handler, seller
2. *n* spy

agree 1. *vb* consent, assent, concur, accept, accede (antonyms: argue, object)
2. *vb* match, correspond, coincide, harmonize, accord, jibe, suit

air 1. *n* sky, heaven, atmosphere, stratosphere, troposphere, space
2. *n* breath, ventilation, oxygen, wind
3. *n* quality, appearance
4. *vb* broadcast, play, say

alike 1. *adj* similar, like, analogous, comparable, equivalent, parallel, close, akin, same (antonym: different)
2. *adv* similarly, likewise, comparably, analogously

alive *adj* living, live, animate, animated, vital, viable, quick, organic, lively, active (antonym: dead)

all 1. *n, pron* everything, everyone, everybody, sum, whole, totality, total
2. *adj* every, entire, each, complete, whole, total
3. *adv* completely

alone *adj* lone, solitary, isolated, unaccompanied, unattended, solo, single-handed, lonely, single

alternate 1. *vb* reciprocate, oscillate, fluctuate, switch
2. *adj* alternating, every other, periodic
3. *n* substitute, replacement, backup, surrogate, double

ancestor *n* forebear, forefather, progenitor, forerunner, predecessor, antecedent, patriarch, matriarch, elder, parent

angel *n* spirit, sprite, archangel, seraph, cherub

angry *adj* mad, furious, upset, annoyed, irritated, aggravated, exasperated, indignant, irate, infuriated, livid, bitter, sore, cross, belligerent, violent

animal 1. *n* creature, beast, brute, being, organism, monster
2. *adj* bestial, beastly, brutish

announcement *n* declaration, notice, notification, proclamation, report, statement, pronouncement, news, revelation, bulletin, message, tidings, advertisement

answer 1. *n* reply, response, retort, rejoinder, riposte, reaction, reciprocation (antonym: question)
2. *n* solution, key, result, explanation, resolution, product (antonyms: problem, question)
3. *vb* reply, respond, retort, acknowledge, echo, counter, react, reciprocate (antonym: question)
4. *vb* solve
5. *vb* satisfy

anticipate 1. *vb* foresee, expect, look forward to, predict
2. *vb* hope

anxious 1. *adj* worried, apprehensive, uneasy, disturbed, insecure, afraid, nervous, tense
2. *adj* eager

anyway *adv* anyhow, nevertheless, nonetheless, however, regardless, notwithstanding, still

apology *n* excuse, acknowledgment, regrets, explanation

apparently 1. *adv* evidently, seemingly, presumably, supposedly, reputedly, probably
2. *adv* clearly, obviously, plainly, patently

appear 1. *vb* emerge, arise, rise, surface, materialize, come into view, show up, turn up, form

appointment 1. *n* selection, nomination, election, designation, assignment, delegation, installation, investiture, ordination, choice
2. *n* meeting, visit
3. *n* profession

appreciate 1. *vb* value, prize, cherish, treasure, relish, savor, respect
2. *vb* thank, enjoy, welcome
3. *vb* understand

approach 1. *vb* come near, draw near, near, advance, loom, gravitate toward, come
2. *vb* address, accost, speak to, talk (antonym: avoid)
3. *n* coming, arrival, appearance, advent, entry
4. *n* method, treatment

approve 1. *vb* endorse, support, authorize, sanction, certify, ratify, validate, legalize, affirm, agree, back
2. *vb* accept, favor, applaud, recommend, acclaim, commend, appreciate

approximate 1. *adj* rough, inexact, estimated, close, near, ballpark, general
2. *vb* estimate
3. *vb* resemble

argue 1. *vb* quarrel, debate, dispute, disagree, bicker, squabble, quibble,

wrangle, fight (antonym: agree)
2. *vb* claim, maintain, plead, assert, contend, allege, charge, protest

aristocracy *n* nobility, gentry, elite, upper class, society, high society, jet set, rich

arrange 1. *vb* organize, sort, classify, order, file, systematize, categorize, determine, array, structure, place, rank, orient, orientate, adjust, straighten
2. *vb* plan, devise, set up, schedule

art *n* skill, craft, technique, artistry, craftsmanship, creativity, artifice, talent

ask *vb* inquire, request, question, interrogate, query, quiz, examine, interview, grill, petition, apply, beg

assortment *n* variety, mix, selection, collection, compilation, array, miscellany, range, series, gamut, medley, potpourri, hash, pile, mess

assume 1. *vb* presume, postulate, presuppose, surmise, gather, guess, believe, pretend
2. *vb* adopt, bear

attack 1. *vb* invade, assault, charge, ambush, waylay, mug, storm, raid, beseige, harry, assail, ravage, bombard, strike, fight, argue, pillage (antonym: protect)
2. *n* assault, raid, invasion, charge, offensive, offense, incursion, strike, sally, sortie, foray, onset, onslaught, counterattack, operation, sack

attention 1. *n* concentration, awareness, alertness, thought, consideration, diligence
2. *n* notice

attractive *adj* appealing, fascinating, captivating, magnetic, alluring, inviting, desirable, intriguing, charming, charismatic, winning, pretty, pleasant

audience *n* spectators, viewers, onlookers, readers, listeners, patrons, congregation, gallery, meeting

automatic 1. *adj* automated, mechanical, mechanized, motorized, self-starting, self-acting, computerized
2. *adj* habitual, involuntary, instinctive, mechanical, spontaneous, reflex, unintentional

available *adj* accessible, usable, convenient, handy, ready

average 1. *adj* unexceptional, mediocre, unremarkable, standard, routine, medium, modest, common, normal
2. *n* mean, median, midpoint, standard, medium, par, norm

avoid *vb* shun, dodge, evade, shirk, duck, sidestep, elude, avert, bypass, circumvent, escape

awesome 1. *adj* amazing, impressive, astonishing, miraculous, terrific, sensational, grand, great
2. *adj* scary

awful *adj* terrible, horrible, dreadful, dire, ghastly, appalling, wretched, grievous, disagreeable, atrocious, outrageous, disgraceful, hateful, odious, bad, gruesome

axis *n* pivot, fulcrum, swivel, hinge, middle

B

bad 1. *adj* evil, sinful, naughty, infamous, villainous, nefarious, incorrigible, disreputable, wicked, improper, mischievous, dishonest, immoral (antonym: good)
2. *adj* unpleasant, disagreeable, undesirable, objectionable, miserable, lousy, nasty, offensive, abominable, repulsive, detestable, despicable, vile, nauseating, sickening, unsavory, disgusting, obnoxious, distasteful, awful
3. *adj* rotten, spoiled, rancid, decayed, putrid, moldy, stale
4. *adj* sad
5. *adj* unhealthy
6. *adj* wrong

bag 1. *n* sack, pouch, purse, handbag, pocketbook, satchel, tote bag, tote, backpack, pack, knapsack, fanny pack, container, luggage, wallet
2. *n* base
3. *vb* catch

balance 1. *n* stability, equilibrium, footing, poise
2. *n* symmetry, harmony, counterbalance, proportion, equilibrium
3. *n* remainder
4. *vb* stabilize, counterbalance, steady, poise, counterpoise, neutralize, equalize, redeem, compensate, coordinate, offset

band 1. *n* group
2. *n* group, orchestra, ensemble, combo
3. *n* stripe, ribbon, belt, girdle, sash, tape, border, strip, streak, seam, vein, row, zone, string

bang 1. *n* crash, crack, pop, boom, blast, explosion, report, thud, detonation, clang, rumble, clap, thunder, noise, knock
2. *vb* rattle, clatter, clash, clank, bump, knock, hit, collide

barrier *n* obstacle, obstruction, hindrance, hurdle, difficulty, impediment, barricade, roadblock, blockade, palisade, clog, divider

base 1. *n* foundation, bottom, support, footing, foot, root, floor (antonym: top)
2. *n* basis
3. *n* headquarters, home, home base, base camp, camp, station, terminal
4. *n* plate, goal, bag, sack
5. *vb* found, ground, predicate, establish
6. *vb* locate, station, post, situate

basic *adj* elemental, elementary, fundamental, staple, rudimentary, primitive, introductory, primary, necessary

basis *n* foundation, support, justification, grounds, authority, underpinning, raison d'être, cornerstone, rudiment, base, cause

bear 1. *vb* endure, stand, tolerate, abide, stomach, suffer, accept, brook, take, shoulder, assume, undertake, experience
2. *vb* carry
3. *vb* support, afford

4. *vb* give

beautiful *adj* gorgeous, glamorous, exquisite, beauteous, elegant, stunning, ravishing, dazzling, magnificent, pretty (antonym: ugly)

because *conj* since, due to, for, as, on account of

before 1. *adv* previously, formerly, earlier, already, beforehand, yet
2. *prep* prior to, ahead of, preceding, until

beginning *n* origin, source, outset, onset, commencement, initiation, inauguration, start, birth, conception, genesis, infancy, threshold, front (antonyms: finish, conclusion)

behavior 1. *n* conduct, manners, etiquette, decorum, bearing
2. *n* performance, function, operation, execution

belief 1. *n* conviction, opinion, view, notion, mind, instinct, hunch, suspicion, attitude, sentiment, theory, idea, feeling, perspective
2. *n* faith, trust, confidence, credit, credence, understanding, certainty
3. *n* creed, doctrine, dogma, credo, principle, religion, philosophy, superstition

believe 1. *vb* accept, think, hold, deem, trust, acknowledge, affirm, view (antonym: deny)
2. *vb* guess

belong *vb* fit, go, fit in, pertain, apply, relate, concern

bend 1. *vb* twist, curve, wind, arch, warp, flex, buckle, bow, droop, veer, meander, thread, contort, distort, turn, slant (antonym: straighten)
2. *vb* bow, curtsy, genuflect, stoop, kneel, crouch, squat, duck, hunch, slouch, slump
3. *n* twist, kink, crimp, curl, tangle, curve, corner

beside *prep* next to, alongside, adjoining, adjacent to, against, near, with

best 1. *adj* finest, choicest, first, prime, premium, optimum, preeminent, leading, unparalleled, unsurpassed, superlative, foremost, ultimate, supreme, top, upper, good (antonym: worst)
2. *adv* most, above all (antonym: least)
3. *vb* defeat, exceed

better 1. *adj* finer, greater, preferable, improved, superior, good, best
2. *adj* improved, improving, convalescent, convalescing, healthy
3. *adv* more
4. *vb* exceed
5. *vb* defeat

between *prep* among, amid, amongst, amidst, betwixt, through

big *adj* large, generous, substantial, considerable, giant, stout, stocky, great, huge, heavy, fat, infinite, abundant, high (antonym: small)

bit 1. *n* piece, fragment, particle, scrap, shred, chip, flake, fleck, trifle, snippet, snatch, bite, block, part

2. *n* trace, hint, suggestion, shade, touch, lick, glimmer, dash, pinch, tang, modicum, jot, iota, shred
3. *n* role, act

bite 1. *vb* chew, gnaw, nibble, munch, taste, chomp, nip, snap
2. *n* morsel, taste, mouthful, nibble, scrap, bit, meal

black *adj, n* ebony, jet, sable, raven, inky, pitch-black, coal-black, dark (antonym: white)

blame 1. *vb* censure, criticize, condemn, denounce, accuse, implicate, charge, try, scold (antonym: forgive)
2. *n* guilt

blank 1. *adj* empty, clean
2. *adj* expressionless, vacuous, impassive, vacant, deadpan, poker-faced

bleak *adj* dreary, desolate, somber, grim, depressing, drear, hopeless, cheerless, gloomy, oppressive, dismal, dour, sad, sterile, pessimistic

block 1. *n* piece, chunk, cube, cake, slice, slab, bar, hunk, wedge, bit, part
2. *n* neighborhood, building
3. *vb* hide
4. *vb* bar

blush *vb* flush, redden, color, glow

boast 1. *vb* brag, gloat, crow, show off, vaunt, swagger, exult
2. *n* brag, bragging, vaunt, claim, assertion, bluster, swagger, bravado

body 1. *n* build, physique, frame, anatomy, figure, form, torso, trunk

2. *n* corpse, carcass, cadaver, remains, skeleton, bones
3. *n* human being
4. *n* group
5. *n* matter
6. *n* density

book *n* volume, publication, text, paperback, hardcover, work, tome, manual, handbook, audiobook, manuscript, script, libretto, pamphlet

border 1. *n* frontier, boundary, borderland, edge, circumference, band
2. *vb* abut, adjoin, neighbor, bound, skirt, flank, join

bored *adj* uninterested, jaded, blasé, tired

boss 1. *n* chief, leader, head, director, employer, foreman, manager, supervisor, superior, captain, commander, skipper, principal, chairperson

bother 1. *vb* annoy, vex, tease, plague, pester, needle, aggravate, irk, nag, hound, badger, harass, bug, irritate, chafe, rankle, disturb, worry

brave 1. *adj* courageous, heroic, fearless, valiant, valorous, gallant, bold, stalwart, daring, audacious, intrepid, dauntless, undaunted, adventurous, adventuresome, plucky, dashing (antonym: afraid)
2. *vb* face

break 1. *vb* crack, shatter, smash, fracture, split, snap, crash, splinter, burst, rupture, crush, squash, chip, destroy, explode, separate

2. *vb* disobey

3. *vb* defeat

4. *n* fracture, split, crack, rift, breach, gap, opening, chip, schism

5. *n* pause, recess, intermission, breather, respite, delay, interlude, interruption, lull, hiatus, suspension, disruption, vacation, rest, truce

6. *n* luck

breathe 1. *vb* inhale, exhale, respire, expire, pant, gasp, wheeze, puff, huff, gulp, mumble

2. *vb* live

bridge 1. *n* span, overpass, catwalk, gangway, gangplank, viaduct

2. *n* link

3. *vb* cross, connect, span, join

bright 1. *adj* brilliant, glowing, radiant, sunny, dazzling, glaring, blazing, intense, luminous, colorful, gay, vivid, flashy, fair, shiny (antonyms: dim, dull)

2. *adj* happy

3. *adj* smart

bring *vb* fetch, deliver, lead, conduct, escort, take, lead, carry, pull

broken 1. *adj* cracked, shattered, fractured, damaged, defective, faulty, malfunctioning, disabled, broken-down, down, unusable, out of order, useless

2. *adj* tame

brush 1. *n* underbrush, undergrowth, shrubbery, thicket, bushes, hedge

2. *n* meeting

3. *vb* clean, sweep, rub, scrub

4. *vb* comb

build 1. *vb* construct, erect, assemble, raise, fabricate, fashion, form, invent, make (antonym: destroy)

2. *vb* strengthen

3. *n* body

burn 1. *vb* blaze, flare, incinerate, scorch, singe, sear, char, glow, smoke, cook

2. *vb* hurt

business 1. *n* industry, commerce, trade, traffic, manufacturing, finance, economics

2. *n* affair, matter, concern, transaction, job

3. *n* company, firm, establishment, corporation, enterprise, outfit, partnership, concern, factory

but 1. *conj* however, although, though, yet, except, nevertheless

2. *prep* except, besides, save, excluding, barring

buy 1. *vb* purchase, pay for, barter, shop, get, hire

2. *n* bargain

C

call 1. *vb* summon, beckon, invite, page, accost, welcome, visit

2. *vb, n* yell

3. *vb* phone, telephone, ring, dial, buzz

4. *vb* name

5. *n* attraction

6. *n* reason

calm 1. *adj* peaceful, serene,

tranquil, placid, undisturbed, untroubled, composed, self-possessed, relaxed, poised, quiet, gentle

2. *n* quiet, tranquility, peacefulness, serenity, stillness, composure, silence, hush (antonym: activity)

3. *vb* quiet, relax, soothe, ease, comfort, compose, lull (antonym: excite)

candidate *n* nominee, aspirant, applicant, office-seeker, front-runner, dark horse, favorite son, contestant

careful 1. *adj* painstaking, thorough, exact, accurate, particular, precise, meticulous, conscientious, studious, scrupulous, nice

2. *adj* cautious, wary, prudent, concerned, circumspect, politic, discreet, judicious, guarded (antonym: thoughtless)

carry 1. *vb* move, transport, convey, bear, cart, pack, haul, transfer, tote, take

2. *vb* sell

3. *vb* support

castle *n* fortress, fort, garrison, fortification, stronghold, citadel, keep, donjon, palace

catch 1. *vb* capture, trap, grasp, take, bag, snag, clasp, snare, ensnare, entangle, mire, enslave, seize, arrest (antonym: free)

2. *vb* pass, overtake, outrun, outstrip

3. *vb* contract, develop, come down with, incur, get

4. *n* grab, snag, scoop

5. *n* clasp, lock

6. *n* trap

cause 1. *vb* produce, create, effect, generate, prompt, inspire, motivate, engender, start, make, do

2. *n* origin, source, stimulus, basis, reason

3. *n* principle, conviction, movement

celebrate 1. *vb* observe, commemorate, keep, solemnize, honor, praise

2. *vb* rejoice, carouse, revel, party

ceremony 1. *n* service, ritual, rite, celebration, tradition, commemoration, festival

2. *n* formality, pomp, solemnity, protocol

certain 1. *adj* sure, positive, confident, definite, assertive, forceful, vehement, self-confident, assured, convinced

2. *adj* undeniable, unquestionable, definite, absolute, inevitable, inescapable, unavoidable, reliable, conclusive, infallible

3. *adj* special

4. *adj* reliable

chance 1. *n* fate, fortune, luck, destiny, lot, accident, coincidence, happenstance, serendipity

2. *n* possibility

3. *n* opportunity

4. *adj* arbitrary, accidental

5. *vb* happen

change 1. *vb* alter, vary, modify,

transform, convert, mutate, shift, innovate, correct, adjust, distort, tinker

2. *vb* switch, exchange, replace, interchange, substitute, swap, reverse, invert, transpose, trade

3. *n* alteration, variation, shift, deviation, evolution, mutation, transformation, revolution, modification, metamorphosis, transition, vicissitude

channel *n* trough, chute, gutter, sluice, shaft, ramp, slide, groove, furrow, trench, rut, ditch, moat, aqueduct, canal, waterway, artery, pipe, course

cheap 1. *adj* inexpensive, reasonable, affordable, economical, low-priced, cut-rate, budget (antonym: expensive)

2. *adj* inferior, shoddy, mediocre, second-rate, chintzy

3. *adj* thrifty, frugal, prudent, stingy, miserly, tight-fisted, penny-pinching, cheeseparing, penurious, tight

cheat 1. *vb* trick, deceive, swindle, chisel, hoodwink, beguile, bluff, defraud, dupe, con, gyp, prey on, fool

2. *n* cheater, swindler, quack, charlatan, fraud, shyster, imposter, fake, humbug, criminal, hypocrite

childish *adj* childlike, infantile, immature, juvenile, puerile, sophomoric, young

choice 1. *n* alternative, option, selection, pick, preference, way, recourse, vote, voice, preference

2. *adj* good, favorite, special

choose *vb* select, pick, elect, opt, name, take, designate, vote, decide, prefer (antonym: exclude)

circle 1. *n* ring, loop, hoop, disk, coil, circuit, circumference, perimeter, periphery, revolution, orbit, round

2. *vb* ring

citizen *n* inhabitant, subject, native, resident, national, denizen, occupant

civilization 1. *n* cultivation, culture, enlightenment, refinement, breeding, polish, progress

2. *n* people

clarity *n* clearness, lucidity, simplicity, transparency, definition, focus, sharpness, resolution

clean 1. *vb* wash, cleanse, rinse, scrub, scrape, scour, launder, bathe, brush, tidy, purify, sterilize, filter, shine, sweep

2. *adj* spotless, washed, unblemished, unused, unsoiled, fresh, blank, pristine, immaculate, neat, sterile (antonym: dirty)

climb 1. *vb* scale, clamber, scramble, crawl, ascend

2. *n* ascent, ascension, rise, growth, slant

clothes *n* clothing, dress, apparel, wardrobe, garments, attire, garb, vestments, finery, habit

cold *adj* frosty, icy, freezing, frigid, arctic, polar, antarctic, raw, cool (antonym: hot)

collide *vb* crash, smash, impact,

sideswipe, rear-end, hit, knock

colony 1. *n* possession, dependency, settlement, satellite, state, country
2. *n* herd

come *vb* arrive, reach, appear, attain, approach, descend (antonym: go)

comfortable 1. *adj* cozy, snug, comfy, restful, homey, roomy, spacious (antonym: uncomfortable)
2. *adj* rich

committee *n* board, council, panel, commission, subcommittee, delegation, mission, cabinet, assembly

common 1. *adj* ordinary, typical, familiar, everyday, widespread, average, unpretentious, humble, commonplace, pedestrian, popular, prevalent, general, normal, usual, plain (antonym: strange)
2. *adj* vulgar, coarse, commonplace, crass, crude, banal, plebeian, cheap, dirty
3. *adj* communal, mutual, joint, collective, collaborative, shared, unanimous, public
4. *n* park

compare *vb* contrast, juxtapose, parallel, liken, match, correlate, study, distinguish

compete *vb* contend, rival, play, contest, vie, fight, face

complain *vb* protest, gripe, grouch, grumble, whine, nag, fuss, moan, groan, mumble, object

complete 1. *adj* entire, full, total, whole, absolute, utter, uncut, intact, unbroken, exhaustive, thorough, unabridged, uncensored, all, comprehensive, perfect
2. *vb* finish

concentrate 1. *vb* focus, devote, attend, meditate, think, study
2. *vb* focus, converge, consolidate, condense, compress, intensify, thicken, distill, gather

conclusion 1. *n* inference, assumption, deduction, decision (antonym: beginning)
2. *n* afterword, epilogue, postscript, postlude, coda (antonym: introduction)
3. *n* finish

confuse *vb* perplex, puzzle, bewilder, confound, complicate, baffle, disconcert, disorient, befuddle, abash, stymie, mystify, throw, stump

conservative *adj* conventional, traditional, orthodox, moderate, reactionary, right-wing, illiberal, stuffy (antonym: liberal)

consider *vb* reflect, weigh, entertain, contemplate, study, think

contain 1. *vb* hold, include, consist of, comprise, accommodate, carry, embody
2. *vb* restrain, limit, suppress, curb, quell, quash, quench, control, repress, swallow, stop, extinguish, prevent

continue 1. *vb* last, endure, remain, persist, persevere, carry on, proceed

2. *vb* resume, recommence, renew, pick up, start

contradict *vb* deny, refute, challenge, dispute, object, discredit

control 1. *vb* command, direct, manage, dominate, subject, regulate, engineer, tame, captain, cope, handle, harness, govern, lead, contain
2. *vb* contain
3. *n* rule, discipline

cool 1. *adj* chilly, chill, brisk, fresh, bracing, nippy, cold
2. *adj* remote, aloof, distant, reserved, chilly, impersonal, calm, apathetic, unfriendly
3. *adj* excellent, all right, fashionable, good
4. *vb* chill, refrigerate, freeze, congeal, fan

copy 1. *n* reproduction, facsimile, photocopy, likeness, duplicate
2. *vb* reproduce, imitate

correct 1. *adj* accurate, right, exact, precise, true, faultless, flawless, authentic, faithful, factual, perfect (antonym: wrong)
2. *adj* respectable, decent, proper, fitting, appropriate, seemly, decorous, becoming, fit, prim
3. *vb* remedy, rectify, revise, edit, amend, emend, reconcile, improve, reform, redress, fix, adjust, perfect, change
4. *vb* punish

country 1. *n* nation, republic, kingdom, dominion, realm, commonwealth, land, domain, homeland, fatherland, motherland, state, colony
2. *n* countryside, landscape, hinterland, wilderness, wild, backwoods, frontier, bush
3. *n* music

courage *n* bravery, valor, fortitude, boldness, spirit, gallantry, heroism, daring, audacity, nerve, mettle, grit, stomach

course 1. *n* path, route, direction, heading, bearing, way, itinerary
2. *n* track, racetrack, trail, road
3. *n* class, subject, seminar, program, major, minor, colloquium, elective

court 1. *n* courtyard, square, quadrangle, quad, atrium, patio, plaza, piazza, cloister
2. *n* field
3. *n* tribunal, law court, bench, bar, judiciary, forum
4. *n* courthouse, courtroom
5. *n* retinue, entourage, cortege, royal household, attendants
6. *vb* woo, date, romance, flirt, love

cover 1. *vb* cover up, blanket, carpet, spread, coat, overspread, surface, pave, flag, wrap, protect, plate
2. *vb* hide
3. *n* top
4. *n* blanket, wrapper
5. *n* protection

crime *n* offense, violation, sin, evil, wrong, wrongdoing, misdeed, trespass, transgression, infraction, felony, misdemeanor, theft, treason, murder

crowd *n* mob, multitude, host, throng, army, legion, horde, swarm, flock, band, group, troop

cry 1. *vb* weep, sob, wail, bawl, whimper, whine, moan, groan
2. *n, vb* shout, scream, howl, screech, bellow, shriek, roar, whoop, squeal, bay, yowl, wail, squawk, noise, yell, bark

curious 1. *adj* inquisitive, prying, nosy, inquiring, meddlesome
2. *adj* strange

cut 1. *vb* chop, slice, dice, mince, shred, grate, carve, cleave, gouge, hew, hack, lacerate, amputate, rip, peel
2. *vb* trim, shave, clip, snip, shear, prune, mow, reap
3. *vb* condense, decrease
4. *n* gash, slash, wound, injury, incision, laceration, scrape, scratch, nick, gouge, cleft, notch, slit, rip, hole, sore

cute *adj* adorable, charming, quaint, cutesy, pretty

D

damage 1. *n* destruction, wreckage, wear, devastation, desolation, ruin, havoc, mayhem, injury, sabotage, decay, harm
2. *vb* impair, mar, deface, scratch, scrape, scar, disfigure, deform, distort, hurt, break, destroy

dangerous *adj* harmful, perilous, hazardous, unsafe, risky, treacherous, precarious, explosive, deadly, destructive (antonym: safe)

dark 1. *adj* gloomy, murky, dusky, shady, unlit, somber, overcast, pitch-black, black, opaque, dim
2. *adj* brunette, brown, tan, black, swarthy, sable, ebony
3. *n* darkness, dusk, gloom, blackness, shade, shadow, night

dead 1. *adj* deceased, departed, late, lifeless, extinct, defunct, inanimate (antonym: alive)
2. *adj* inert, still, stagnant, motionless, calm
3. *adj* tired
4. *adv* completely
5. *n* casualty

decay 1. *vb* deteriorate, disintegrate, crumble, decompose, wear, rot, molder, spoil, putrefy, corrode, destroy
2. *n* deterioration, degeneration, decomposition, spoilage, disrepair, disintegration, corrosion, damage

decide *vb* settle, resolve, determine, rule, conclude, reconcile, negotiate, mediate, arbitrate, judge, adjudge, convict, choose

decorate 1. *vb* adorn, beautify, ornament, embellish, trim, garnish, bedeck, redecorate, refurbish, festoon
2. *vb* praise

decrease 1. *vb* lessen, diminish, abate, decline, wane, subside, ebb, dwindle, taper, shrink, shrivel, reduce, depress, lower, slash, curtail, cut, condense, weaken
2. *n* drop

defeat 1. *vb* conquer, beat, overcome, surmount, overpower, vanquish, best, better, top, break, overthrow, throw, upset, down, whip, crush, subdue, win
2. *n* loss, downfall, failure, conquest, destruction, rout, upset, beating, thrashing (antonym: victory)

delay 1. *vb* postpone, defer, put off, deter, stall, procrastinate, wait, hesitate
2. *vb* hamper, detain, impede, hinder, retard, prevent
3. *n* break

department *n* section, division, branch, bureau, agency, chapter, subsidiary, affiliate, field, business, job, arm

departure 1. *n* exit, going, leaving, withdrawal, farewell, embarkation, exodus, escape
2. *n* deviation, divergence, digression, aberration, irregularity, change, difference

depend 1. *vb* trust, rely, count on, believe
2. *vb* hang, hinge, rest, turn

depression 1. *n* dent
2. *n* desolation, despair, despondency, dejection, sorrow, misery
3. *n* recession, slump, decline, downturn, crash

describe *vb* characterize, define, depict, represent, recount, detail, explain, draw

deserve *vb* merit, earn, warrant, justify, rate

destination *n* end, terminus, terminal, station, address, target

destroy *vb* wreck, spoil, demolish, ruin, annihilate, damage, devastate, ravage, raze, level, blight, abolish, break, mutilate (antonym: build)

detail 1. *n* particular, trait, feature, factor, specific, peculiarity, fact, point
2. *vb* specify, describe

dialect *n* idiom, vernacular, patois, slang, lingo, argot, jargon, cant, creole, pidgin, accent, language

die 1. *vb* decease, expire, pass away, pass on, perish, succumb, depart, starve (antonym: live)
2. *n* form

different 1. *adj* distinct, other, else, another, separate, dissimilar, unlike, irregular, uneven, unequal, unique (antonyms: same, similar)
2. *adj* diverse, various, assorted, miscellaneous, disparate, eclectic, assorted, varied, heterogeneous, motley, many
3. *adj* strange

diplomat *n* ambassador, consul, emissary, statesman, attaché, envoy, minister, chargé d'affaires, official

dirty 1. *adj* filthy, grimy, soiled, dingy, grubby, unclean, impure, unsanitary, contaminated, polluted, foul, dusty, squalid, messy (antonym: clean)
2. *adj* obscene, lewd,

pornographic, ribald, vulgar, bawdy, coarse, earthy, salty, risqué, racy, common

3. *vb* soil, stain, sully, pollute, contaminate, infect, defile, tarnish, taint, foul, befoul, smudge, muddy, mess (antonym: clean)

disabled 1. *adj* handicapped, physically challenged, differently abled, impaired, incapacitated

2. *adj* hampered, thwarted, encumbered, deterred, handicapped, disadvantaged, stymied

3. *adj* broken

disagreement *n* contention, friction, discord, strife, dissent, dissension, heresy, argument, contradiction, fight, opposition

disappear *vb* vanish, fade, lift, dissipate, dissolve, evaporate, fizzle, disperse, thin, melt, stop

disappoint *vb* let down, fail, discourage, dishearten, dissatisfy, disillusion, frustrate, sadden

disaster 1. *n* catastrophe, calamity, tragedy, casualty, cataclysm, misfortune, pity, evil, accident, emergency

2. *n* disappointment

discover 1. *vb* detect, unearth, uncover, strike, descry, ferret out, find, notice

2. *vb* learn

disease *n* infection, virus, fever, contagion, blight, syndrome, blight, illness, epidemic

dishonest *adj* untruthful, untrustworthy, deceitful, crooked, lying, deceptive, corrupt, unprincipled, unscrupulous, fake, sly, bad

disobey *vb* defy, disregard, violate, break, misbehave, transgress, rebel, refuse, fight, sin (antonym: obey)

distance 1. *n* stretch, length, interval, gap, way, expanse, extent, measure

2. *n* background

disturb 1. *vb* disarrange, displace, dislocate, disorder, mess, muss, dishevel, rumple, garble, move

2. *vb* interrupt, disrupt, intrude, interfere, impose, bother, distract

3. *vb* agitate, upset, perturb, unnerve, unsettle, disconcert, ruffle, jar, worry, bother

divide 1. *vb* part, split, partition, segment, subdivide, portion, apportion, halve, quarter, zone, cut, separate, share

2. *vb* diverge, branch, fork

3. *vb* arrange

do 1. *vb* accomplish, achieve, carry out, render, act, cause, work

2. *vb* solve

3. *vb* satisfy

document *n* record, certificate, form, file, diploma, citation, affidavit, passport, deed, credentials, manuscript, report, agreement, license, ticket

door *n* doorway, entrance, entry, exit, gate, gateway, access, portal, passage, outlet, opening, mouth, threshold

dream *n* reverie, daydream, trance, daze, spell, stupor, study, swoon, hope

dress 1. *vb* wear, clothe, don, robe, attire, costume, outfit, deck
2. *vb* trim, groom, array, decorate
3. *vb* bandage
4. *n* gown, frock, jumper, sheath, skirt, shift, shirtwaist, pinafore, smock, sari, sarong, muumuu, clothes

drive 1. *vb* steer, maneuver, navigate, pilot, ride, propel, jockey, operate, control
2. *vb* banish
3. *n* trip
4. *n* ambition, energy

drug *n* antibiotic, narcotic, sedative, tranquilizer, painkiller, anesthetic, opiate, hallucinogen, antidepressant, medicine

dry 1. *adj* arid, parched, dehydrated, desiccated, dusty, thirsty, stale (antonym: wet)
2. *adj* dull
3. *adj* droll, wry, deadpan, sardonic, funny
4. *adj* sour
5. *vb* wipe, drain
6. *vb* evaporate, dehydrate, wilt, wither, shrivel, harden

dull 1. *adj* uninteresting, boring, tedious, dreary, monotonous, tiresome, prosaic, humdrum, shallow, deadly, dry, drab, insipid (antonyms: interesting, lively)
2. *adj* slow, stolid, obtuse, dense, unimaginative, square, stupid

3. *adj* blunt, unsharpened (antonym: sharp)
4. *adj* drab, dim, dingy, faded, lackluster, flat, bleak, dark, dim (antonym: bright)

duplicate 1. *n* double, twin, replica, counterpart, equivalent, analogue, parallel, copy, model
2. *vb* repeat, reproduce

duty 1. *n* responsibility, obligation, trust, charge
2. *n* job
3. *n* tax

E

eager *adj* enthusiastic, keen, avid, anxious, ardent, passionate, fervent, exuberant, impatient, ready, ambitious

early 1. *adj* initial, original, first, earliest, pioneering, pioneer, primary, inaugural, introductory, preliminary, incipient, embryonic, developing, nascent (antonym: late)
2. *adj* premature, untimely, precocious, hasty, prompt, sudden (antonym: late)
3. *adj* primitive, primeval, prehistoric, primal, archaic, primordial, old (antonym: modern)

easy *adj* effortless, light, simple, moderate, straightforward, obvious, plain (antonym: hard)

eat 1. *vb* consume, devour, dine, feast, feed, graze, browse, gulp, gobble, wolf, gorge, bolt, prey on

2. *vb* corrode

edge *n* rim, margin, fringe, brink, boundary, verge, brim, lip, hem, periphery, border, circumference, side, shore

educated *adj* literate, learned, knowledgeable, informed, studious, scholarly, erudite, lettered, well-read, well-informed, well-versed, schooled, bookish, smart (antonym: ignorant)

effect 1. *n* result, outcome, consequence, upshot, aftermath, issue, product
2. *n* impact, impression, influence
3. *vb* cause

embarrass *vb* abash, disconcert, rattle, faze, discomfit, fluster, mortify, chagrin, shame

emergency *n* crisis, exigency, extremity, disaster, trouble, accident

emotion *n* sentiment, passion, drama, affect, feeling

emphasize *vb* highlight, feature, stress, accent, accentuate, underscore, underline

empty 1. *adj* vacant, unoccupied, uninhabited, bare, austere, blank, void, devoid, hollow, open, abandoned (antonym: full)
2. *adj* idle, vain, meaningless, hollow
3. *vb* unload, unpack, unwrap, remove, dump out, pour out, clean out, evacuate, vacate, deflate, drain

enemy *n* rival, adversary, antagonist, foe, attacker, assailant, opponent

energy 1. *n* vigor, vitality, life, liveliness, pep, stamina, endurance, vim, drive, get-up-and-go, zip, steam, strength, excitement
2. *n* power, horsepower, pressure, thrust, propulsion, voltage, current, electricity, heat, fuel

enough *adj* ample, sufficient, adequate, abundant, plentiful, plenty, much

enter 1. *vb* penetrate, invade, infiltrate, go, approach, intrude (antonym: leave)
2. *vb* board, mount, embark, entrain, enplane (antonym: leave)
3. *vb* join

enthusiasm *n* passion, zeal, fervor, zest, ardor, eagerness, exuberance, gusto, pleasure, excitement, ambition

envy 1. *vb* desire, covet, resent, grudge, begrudge, want
2. *n* jealousy, covetousness, resentment, spite, desire, malice, greed

equal 1. *adj* same, fair
2. *n* peer, fellow, mate, match, compeer, duplicate

erase *vb* obliterate, delete, scratch, eradicate, expunge, efface, abolish

escape 1. *vb* flee, elude, evade, dodge, break out, bolt, elope, avoid, leave
2. *n* flight, getaway, evasion, desertion, deliverance, rescue, departure

estimate 1. *vb* calculate, evaluate, approximate, reckon, figure,

gauge, assess, judge, appraise, guess
2. *n* approximation, evaluation, appraisal, assessment, estimation, bid, quotation, quote, comparison, budget

event 1. *n* incident, occurrence, episode, circumstance, occasion, happening, phenomenon, actuality, fact
2. *n* milestone, landmark, breakthrough, achievement, experience, adventure, ceremony, disaster
3. *n* game

exaggerate *vb* overstate, overdo, inflate, embellish, embroider, elaborate, gild, magnify, dramatize

examine 1. *vb* investigate, scrutinize, inspect, probe, scan, study, look
2. *vb* test, quiz, interrogate, ask

example *n* instance, case, illustration, specimen, sample, representation, representative, model

excellence *n* perfection, faultlessness, superiority, greatness, distinction, eminence, majesty

excite *vb* stimulate, exhilarate, agitate, thrill, energize, arouse, galvanize, enliven, fan (antonym: calm)

exclude *vb* eliminate, suspend, reject, omit, eject, skip, neglect, ignore, overlook, miss, remove, rid, banish, bar, forbid, forget

expensive *adj* costly, invaluable, precious, dear, high-priced, overpriced, extravagant, upscale, valuable, rich (antonym: cheap)

experience 1. *n* background, training, knowledge, skill, know-how, expertise, knowledge, wisdom, event
2. *vb* undergo, encounter, endure, live through, bear

expert 1. *n* authority, specialist, master, virtuoso, ace, connoisseur
2. *adj* proficient, skilled, masterly, adroit, ace, versed, well-versed, able, smart

explain *vb* clarify, interpret, justify, demonstrate, elucidate, illustrate, illuminate, exemplify, expound, show, treat, solve, describe

explode *vb* erupt, discharge, detonate, blow up, burst, break

F

face 1. *n* features, visage, countenance, expression, profile, appearance
2. *n* side
3. *vb* oppose, confront, defy, brave, challenge, encounter, bear, compete, fight (antonym: retreat)

fair 1. *adj* just, impartial, equal, unbiased, equitable, objective, unprejudiced, neutral, nonpartisan, detached, impersonal, right
2. *adj* satisfactory, acceptable, adequate, mediocre, decent
3. *adj* clear, sunny, bright, pleasant, mild, bright (antonym: cloudy)
4. *adj* blond, blonde, light, white, ivory, creamy, bleached, pale
5. *adj* pretty

6. *n* carnival

faithful 1. *adj* loyal, true, devoted, steadfast, constant, trusty, trustworthy, resolute, staunch, fast, unfailing, unshaken, committed, tenacious, reliable, religious (antonym: unfaithful)
2. *adj* correct

fake 1. *adj* false, artificial, imitation, dummy, ersatz, counterfeit, spurious, phony, bogus, sham, mock, dishonest (antonym: real)
2. *n* phony, counterfeit, forgery, imitation, dummy, copy
3. *n* cheat
4. *vb* forge, counterfeit, falsify, imitate, pretend

fall 1. *vb* drop, collapse, plunge, topple, tumble, plummet, slump, plump, crumple, subside, slip, lapse, sink, set, descend, trip, lose
2. *n* tumble, spill, dive, nosedive, drop
3. *n* wig

family 1. *n* relative, relation, kin, people, kindred, lineage, clan, tribe, stock, strain, ancestry
2. *adj* familial, domestic, home, homey, household, residential

famous *adj* famed, noted, prominent, renowned, eminent, notorious, celebrated, illustrious, distinguished, well-known, popular, important, great

far 1. *adj* distant, remote, faraway, far-flung, removed, outlying, yonder
2. *adv* considerably, incomparably, notably, greatly, much

farm 1. *n* ranch, homestead, plantation, spread, farmstead
2. *vb* till, harvest, garden, grow

fashion 1. *n* style, trend, fad, craze, rage, mode, vogue, thing
2. *vb* make, form, build

fast 1. *adj* rapid, quick, speedy, swift, fleet, hasty, hurried, prompt, cursory, perfunctory, snap, sudden (antonym: slow)
2. *adj* faithful
3. *adj* tight
4. *adv* quickly

fat 1. *adj* plump, obese, stout, overweight, corpulent, portly, chubby, brawny, husky, heavyset, stocky, pudgy, squat, big, heavy
2. *n* oil, lard, shortening, tallow, suet, grease

favorite 1. *adj* preferred, favored, pet, choice, best-liked, popular
2. *n* darling, pet, precious, ideal, lover
3. *n* preference

fear 1. *n* alarm, fright, dread, terror, panic, horror, phobia, anxiety, apprehension, foreboding, dismay, consternation, scare, worry
2. *vb* flinch, cower, tremble, quail, quake, dread

feast 1. *n* banquet, fiesta, repast, meal, party
2. *vb* eat

feeling 1. *n* sense, sensation, perception, feel, touch, quality
2. *n* sensitivity, sentimentality, intuition, instinct, heart, soul, warmth, emotion, impulse

3. *n* belief

feminine *adj* female, ladylike, womanly, matronly, effeminate, motherly (antonym: masculine)

few *adj* several, couple, scant, scanty, negligible, sporadic (antonym: many)

field 1. *n* meadow, pasture, clearing, glade, plot, hayfield, cornfield, wheatfield, farmland, pen
2. *n* playing field, athletic field, diamond, gridiron, arena, track, court, stadium, coliseum, gymnasium
3. *n* airfield, airport, battlefield, battleground
4. *n* subject, area, sphere, realm, discipline, province, arena, bailiwick, domain, orbit, department, profession, specialty

fight 1. *vb* battle, struggle, wrestle, grapple, combat, clash, conflict, war, brawl, feud, duel, skirmish, scrap, strive, resist, argue, attack, compete, face
2. *n* battle, engagement, struggle, war, action, strife, conflict, hostilities, warfare, combat, skirmish, confrontation, encounter, violence, competition, game
3. *n* altercation, clash, scuffle, tussle, scrap, melee, brawl, feud, duel, showdown, fray, rumble, argument, disturbance
4. *n* defiance, resistance, opposition, struggle

finally 1. *adv* conclusively, decisively, irrevocably, permanently, certainly
2. *adv* eventually, ultimately, lastly

finish 1. *vb* complete, end, terminate, conclude, attain, expire, wind up, finalize, clinch, use up, dissolve, disband, stop, use, climax (antonym: start)
2. *n* end, conclusion, ending, finale, completion, termination, culmination, death, fulfillment
3. *n* shine, polish, paint, varnish, shellac, lacquer, stain, wax

fire 1. *n* flame, blaze, conflagration, combustion, campfire, bonfire, pyre, inferno, holocaust, fireplace
2. *n* gunfire, shooting, firing, shelling, bombardment
3. *vb* shoot
4. *vb* dismiss, discharge, terminate, lay off, let go (antonym: hire)

firm 1. *adj* rigid, hard, solid, stiff, inflexible, steady, compact, dense, tough, hard, thick
2. *n* business

fix 1. *vb* repair, mend, patch, restore, renovate, renew, rebuild, overhaul, recondition, service, adjust, correct, tinker
2. *vb* sterilize
3. *n* trouble

flexible *adj* bendable, limber, supple, lithe, malleable, elastic, pliable, plastic, soft, resilient, pliant, limp

flood 1. *n* deluge, torrent, inundation, cascade, rain, storm
2. *n* river, surge, current, rush, flow, stream, tide, wave, fountain
3. *n* barrage, hail, volley, spate,

deluge, torrent, storm
4. *vb* inundate, overflow, submerge, drown, engulf, swamp, overwhelm, flow

fly 1. *vb* soar, glide, float, drift, wing, hover, sail, flutter
2. *vb* hurry
3. *n* housefly, horsefly, bluebottle, blackfly, fruit fly, bug
4. *n* tent

follow 1. *vb* succeed, ensue, supplant, supersede, replace (antonyms: lead, precede)
2. *vb* pursue, chase, trail, track, shadow, hunt, stalk, hound, tail
3. *vb* obey
4. *vb* know, understand

food *n* nourishment, diet, sustenance, edibles, victuals, refreshment, rations, provisions, cuisine, fare, nutrition, fuel, board, meal

fool 1. *n* simpleton, nitwit, idiot, dunce, imbecile, nincompoop, blockhead, moron, oaf, clown, ignoramus, buffoon, dolt, dummy, half-wit, ninny
2. *vb* outsmart, outwit, outfox, delude, cheat

forbid *vb* prohibit, ban, disallow, outlaw, censor, gag, boycott, proscribe, sanction, bar, exclude (antonym: let)

force 1. *vb* require, compel, coerce, make, oblige, obligate, impel, constrain, pressure, insist, order
2. *n* strength
3. *n* army

foreign *adj* alien, imported, exotic, remote, distant, nonnative, immigrant, strange

forever *adv* always, eternally, permanently, perpetually, interminably, endlessly, evermore, regularly

forget *vb* neglect, omit, overlook, disregard, misremember, exclude (antonym: remember)

forgive *vb* excuse, pardon, absolve, acquit, exonerate, clear, vindicate, condone (antonym: blame)

frantic 1. *adj* frenzied, distraught, overwrought, frenetic, desperate, delirious, feverish (antonym: calm)
2. *adj* hectic, chaotic, furious (antonym: calm)

free 1. *vb* release, liberate, emancipate, deliver, discharge, extricate, exempt, loose, loosen, unloose, unloosen, forgive, open
2. *adj* independent, liberated, sovereign, self-governing, autonomous, emancipated, unconfined, unrestrained, unfettered, unshackled, loose, exempt
3. *adj* complimentary, gratis, gratuitous
4. *adj* generous

friend *n* girlfriend, boyfriend, companion, associate, partner, acquaintance, ally, comrade, pal, chum, playmate, buddy (antonyms: enemy, opponent)

full 1. *adj* packed, loaded, laden, filled, crowded, stuffed, replete, sated, brimful, crammed, jammed

(antonym: empty)

2. *adj* complete

funny 1. *adj* laughable, amusing, humorous, witty, hilarious, comical, comic, ridiculous, whimsical, facetious, antic, farcical, zany, ludicrous, dry, foolish, strange

2. *adj* sick

future 1. *n* hereafter, eternity, futurity, tomorrow, morrow, destiny, fate

2. *adj* imminent, impending, pending, forthcoming, upcoming, approaching, prospective, projected

G

game *n* sport, pastime, recreation, contest, match, competition, bout, event, meet, tournament, series, fight

gather 1. *vb* collect, assemble, accumulate, amass, compile, congregate, convene, meet, rendezvous, save, pile

2. *vb* pick, harvest, reap, pluck, garner, glean

3. *vb* assume, infer

general 1. *adj* widespread, extensive, comprehensive, common, usual, universal

2. *adj* approximate

generous 1. *adj* unselfish, charitable, liberal, unsparing, altruistic, kind, free, noble (antonym: selfish)

2. *adj* liberal, handsome, lavish, abundant, big

genius 1. *n* prodigy, virtuoso, mastermind, wizard, wunderkind

2. *n* talent

3. *n* soul

gentle 1. *adj* light, mild, soft, tender, moderate, temperate, calm

2. *adj* friendly, kind

3. *adj* docile, meek, tractable, tame

get 1. *vb* obtain, acquire, gain, win, take, procure, earn, score, catch, receive, seize, find

2. *vb* know

3. *vb* persuade

gift 1. *n* present, donation, grant, contribution, endowment, offering, alms, sacrifice, favor, surprise, boon, inheritance, prize

2. *n* talent

give 1. *vb* present, donate, grant, endow, bestow, impart, award, confer, bequeath, contribute, supply (antonym: receive)

2. *vb* pass, hand, deliver, convey, render, serve, dish out, hand over, hand in, submit, dispense, distribute, inflict, offer

3. *vb* have, hold, stage, act, play

4. *vb* surrender

5. *vb* yield, bear, produce, furnish, make

go 1. *vb* progress, proceed, pass, head, advance, forge ahead, leave, move, travel (antonym: come)

2. *vb* act

3. *vb* belong

4. *vb* happen

5. *n* try

god *n* goddess, deity, divinity,

demigod, immortal, idol, icon, effigy

good 1. *adj* fine, excellent, outstanding, choice, admirable, splendid, rave, favorable, hopeful, positive, suitable, proper, capital, tiptop, fair, great, nice, cool (antonym: bad)
2. *adj* honest, honorable, virtuous, worthy, respectable, reputable, moral, righteous, scrupulous, kind
3. *adj* obedient, well-behaved, dutiful, well-mannered, respectful, obliging, polite (antonym: rude)
4. *n* welfare

government *n* administration, legislature, congress, senate, parliament, assembly, regime, rule

grade *n* class, rank, step, score, standing, position, degree, plateau, level, state, slant

gratitude *n* appreciation, thankfulness, thanks, gratefulness, recognition, acknowledgment

great 1. *adj*, *interj* wonderful, terrific, superb, remarkable, astounding, incredible, spectacular, tremendous, marvelous, fabulous, super, heavenly, good, grand, nice
2. *adj* famous
3. *adj* big

greedy *adj* selfish, possessive, covetous, acquisitive, avaricious, stingy, rapacious, grasping, voracious, insatiable, gluttonous, jealous, predatory

group 1. *n* gang, bunch, crew, pack, set, class, band, body, cluster, ring, bloc, clique, syndicate, junta, troop
2. *n* band

grow 1. *vb* sprout, germinate, develop, expand, increase, mature, ripen, evolve, enlarge, wax, magnify, amplify, heighten, augment, mushroom, multiply, prosper, blossom, strengthen
2. *vb* raise, breed, cultivate, nurture, rear, plant

guarantee 1. *vb* insure, assure, secure, ensure, warrant, certify, promise
2. *n* promise

guess *vb* suppose, think, believe, imagine, suspect, reckon, speculate, surmise, estimate, assume

guide 1. *n* conductor, escort, leader, usher, shepherd, pilot
2. *n* pattern
3. *vb* lead

guilty *adj* culpable, blameworthy, responsible, liable, derelict (antonym: innocent)

gun *n* firearm, weapon, pistol, revolver, sidearm, handgun, rifle, carbine, shotgun, machine gun, musket, flintlock, muzzle loader, blunderbuss, cannon, arms

habit 1. *n* custom, practice, routine, institution, usage, rule
2. *n* dependency, addiction, instinct, reflex, wont, tendency
3. *n* mannerism, affectation, quirk, trait, oddity

4. *n* clothes

habitat *n* environment, habitation, ecosystem, den, house

hang 1. *vb* dangle, drape, suspend, swing, hover, depend
2. *vb* lynch, execute, kill

happen *vb* occur, transpire, chance, go, befall, ensue, arise, recur, exist

happy *adj* glad, cheerful, joyful, joyous, merry, gay, jolly, delighted, gleeful, proud, jovial, high, festive, bright, ecstatic, satisfied, lucky (antonym: sad)

hard 1. *adj* stony, rocky, adamant, firm, tough
2. *adj* difficult, tough, demanding, strenuous, arduous, rigorous, heavy, rough, trying (antonym: easy)
3. *adj* harsh, severe, bitter, austere, stark, stern

harm 1. *n* injury, hurt, loss, impairment, detriment, disadvantage, abuse, damage
2. *vb* hurt, damage

hate 1. *vb* detest, abhor, despise, deplore, loathe, disdain, dislike, abominate, scorn, execrate (antonym: love)
2. *n* hatred

heal *vb* cure, remedy, mend, knit, treat, medicate, nurse, doctor

health *n* fitness, condition, shape, vigor, vitality, haleness, wellness, healthfulness, welfare

heaven 1. *n* paradise, bliss, nirvana, Elysian fields, Elysium, Valhalla, utopia, pleasure

2. *n* air

heavy 1. *adj* cumbersome, hefty, ponderous, massive, weighty, bulky, big (antonym: light)
2. *adj* serious
3. *adj* hard

height 1. *n* altitude, elevation, stature, loftiness, tallness (antonym: depth)
2. *n* top

help 1. *vb* assist, aid, serve, wait on, cooperate, collaborate, team up, succor, benefit, improve, enrich, avail, relieve, support
2. *n* aid, assistance, cooperation, relief, service, support, comfort, generosity, welfare
3. *n* worker

herd *n* flock, pack, swarm, hive, colony, bevy, brood, school, gaggle, pod, group, crowd

hesitate *vb* falter, vacillate, balk, pause, demur, equivocate, waver, stop, delay, wait

hide 1. *vb* conceal, disguise, secrete, bury, withhold, hoard, squirrel (away) (antonym: reveal)
2. *vb* cover (up), camouflage, obscure, eclipse, mask, block, screen, shade, shroud, veil, cloak, cover
3. *n* pelt, skin, fleece, fell, rawhide, chamois, coat

high 1. *adj* tall, lofty, towering, soaring, big
2. *adj* high-pitched, shrill, treble, piping, loud (antonym: low)
3. *adj* important

4. *adj* happy

hill 1. *n* knoll, mound, hillock, foothill, down, dune, bank, ridge, pile, mountain, cliff (antonym: valley)
2. *n* slant

hit 1. *vb* strike, pound, batter, beat, maul, bash, bump, pelt, smash, smack, swat, hammer, buffet, pat, punch, knock, collide, whip
2. *n* blow

hole 1. *n* hollow, cavity, pit, crater, abyss, chasm, crevasse, cave, den, well
2. *n* puncture, perforation, opening, aperture, vent, crack, cleft, fissure, crevice, split, gap, rupture, leak, pore

home 1. *n* house, apartment, condominium, dwelling, residence, abode, domicile, habitation, cabin, cottage, bungalow, chalet, mansion, palace, manor, villa, chateau, den, shack
2. *n* family
3. *n* base
4. *n* hospital

honesty *n* candor, frankness, veracity, truth, virtue

hope 1. *vb* wish, expect, anticipate, aspire, believe, want, intend
2. *n* desire, faith, longing, aspiration, dream, ambition
3. *n* virtue

horizon *n* skyline, limit, range, border

hospital *n* infirmary, clinic, medical center, rehabilitation center, sanatorium, sanitarium, nursing home, home

hot 1. *adj* scalding, boiling, broiling, roasting, sizzling, sweltering, torrid, warm, burning, tropical (antonym: cold)
2. *adj* spicy
3. *adj* fashionable

huge *adj* enormous, immense, gigantic, prodigious, colossal, tremendous, mighty, vast, gross, gargantuan, monstrous, jumbo, mammoth, massive, titanic, big

human being *n* human, person, individual, being, soul, body, mortal, hominid, humanity, man, woman, people

humble 1. *adj* meek, modest, unassuming, unpretentious, self-deprecating, self-effacing, shy (antonym: proud)
2. *adj* common
3. *vb* condescend

hungry *adj* starving, starved, famished, ravenous, underfed, malnourished, undernourished, emaciated, wasted

hunt 1. *vb* fish, shoot, poach, track, follow
2. *vb* search, seek, look, investigate, scour, forage, probe, ransack, rummage, delve, explore, prospect, comb, sift
3. *n* search, investigation, pursuit, chase, quest, exploration, study

hurry 1. *vb* rush, hasten, hustle, speed, race, hurtle, accelerate, quicken, scurry, sally, dash, zip, whiz, zoom, scamper, scuttle, surge, swarm, pour, stampede, storm

2. *n* rush, haste, scramble, stampede, speed

hurt 1. *vb* injure, afflict, damage, wound, bruise, tear, wrench, twist, dislocate, harm, abuse, hit, insult, punish, break, pull

2. *vb* smart, sting, burn, irritate, ache, throb, tingle

hypocrite *n* deceiver, faker, dissembler, quack, con artist, cheat

ice *n* frost, hail, sleet, icicle, ice cube, permafrost

idea *n* thought, concept, impression, inspiration, notion, inkling, belief, theory, plan, suggestion

ignorant *adj* illiterate, uneducated, unlearned, unlettered, unschooled, unread, naive, stupid, unaware (antonym: educated)

illegal *adj* unlawful, illegitimate, illicit, criminal, outlawed, wrongful, prohibited, taboo

illness *n* sickness, ailment, malady, affliction, disorder, infirmity, complaint, disease, nausea

imaginary *adj* unreal, nonexistent, fictional, fictitious, illusory, hypothetical, fanciful, hallucinatory, legendary (antonym: real)

imagine 1. *vb* conceive, picture, see, envision, envisage, visualize, fancy,

fantasize, pretend

2. *vb* guess, think

imitate *vb* copy, mimic, emulate, simulate, parrot, ape, parody, mock, lampoon, satirize, impersonate, caricature

immoral *adj* unethical, unprincipled, shameless, dissolute, degenerate, depraved, perverted, bad, wrong

important 1. *adj* significant, principal, chief, major, main, essential, primary, critical, key, paramount, prime, cardinal, foremost, high, weighty, urgent, necessary, valuable, meaningful, memorable, predominant

2. *adj* influential, prominent, powerful, famous

impossible 1. *adj* inconceivable, unattainable, unthinkable, incomprehensible, useless, illogical, unbelievable

2. *adj* insoluble, unsolvable, inexplicable, unexplainable, unaccountable

3. *adj* intolerable

inability *n* incapability, ineptitude, incompetence, incapacity, inefficacy, impotence, powerlessness, failure

incompetent *adj* incapable, inept, ineffectual, unqualified, unfit, inefficient, unable, amateur, clumsy

inconvenient *adj* awkward, bothersome, troublesome, onerous, irksome, annoying, untimely

infer *vb* deduce, conclude, gather, judge, reason, ascertain, assume, mention

infinite *adj* boundless, unbounded, endless, limitless, unlimited, interminable, countless, immeasurable, inexhaustible, eternal, big (antonym: finite)

innocent 1. *adj* blameless, guiltless, faultless, sinless, pure, chaste, angelic, impeccable (antonym: guilty)
2. *adj* naïve

insane *adj* crazy, mad, crazed, lunatic, psychotic, maniacal, demented, deranged, berserk, paranoid, unbalanced, unhinged, mental (antonym: sane)

insensitive *adj* unfeeling, uncaring, tactless, heartless, hardhearted, coldhearted, callous, unsympathetic, cold-blooded, thoughtless, apathetic, stubborn (antonym: thoughtful)

inside 1. *adj* interior, internal, inner, indoor, innermost, middle
2. *n* middle

insist *vb* demand, require, assert, argue, order, force

instead *adv* rather, alternatively, alternately, preferably

insult 1. *vb* offend, humiliate, slander, defame, malign, smear, slight, snub, outrage, tease, taunt, scorn, abuse, hurt, ridicule
2. *n* affront, offense, indignity, outrage, slander, libel, smear, jeer

intellectual *adj* scholarly, scholastic, educational, academic, cerebral, mental, profound, thoughtful

interesting *adj* fascinating, intriguing, stimulating, engrossing, absorbing, engaging, entertaining, provocative, stirring, compelling, exciting (antonym: dull)

introduce 1. *vb* present, acquaint, familiarize, inform, apprise, broach
2. *vb* preface, precede, start

invent 1. *vb* devise, design, develop, conceive, formulate, originate, contrive, hatch, improvise, ad-lib, build, discover, form, make, start
2. *vb* fabricate, concoct, make up, counterfeit, lie

invisible *adj* imperceptible, indiscernible, undetectable, concealed, hidden, unseen, microscopic, impalpable, ethereal, supernatural, inconspicuous

irony *n* sarcasm, satire, incongruity, parody, humor

island *n* isle, islet, atoll, key, cay, archipelago, holm

jail 1. *n* prison, penitentiary, correctional facility, jailhouse, reformatory, cell, dungeon, brig, stockade
2. *vb* imprison, confine, detain, incarcerate, impound, remand, institutionalize, commit

jealous *adj* envious, resentful,

possessive, begrudging, suspicious, greedy

job *n* task, chore, work, duty, errand, assignment, project, mission, labor, living, profession, function

join 1. *vb* connect, associate, attach, link, fasten, unite, couple, interlock, anchor, bridge, buckle, clasp, clinch, knit, pair, graft, weld, solder, cement, pin, tie, unify, marry
2. *vb* enter, enroll, enlist, register, participate

joke 1. *n* prank, practical joke, gag, caper, antic, trick
2. *n* jest, wisecrack, pun, witticism, quip, one-liner, bon mot, story
3. *vb* jest, quip, banter, spar, kid, tease, josh

judge 1. *n* justice, magistrate, jurist
2. *n* referee, umpire, official, evaluator, reviewer, critic, arbiter
3. *vb* decide
4. *vb* estimate, infer

jump 1. *vb, n* leap, spring, bound, vault, hop, pounce, bounce, jounce, jolt, pop, skip, hurdle, dive, plunge, lunge, dance
2. *vb, n* start, flinch, wince, recoil, twitch, jerk, cringe, cower

justice 1. *n* fairness, impartiality, equity, due process, evenhandedness, honesty, truth, virtue
2. *n* judge

K

keep 1. *vb* have, possess, maintain, retain, preserve, sustain, own
2. *vb* save
3. *vb* fulfill, honor, respect, celebrate
4. *n* board
5. *n* castle, tower

kill *vb* murder, slay, assassinate, dispatch, massacre, butcher, execute, slaughter, exterminate, annihilate, eradicate, martyr, sacrifice, destroy, extinguish, choke

kind 1. *adj* compassionate, considerate, benevolent, well-meaning, charitable, merciful, kindhearted, tenderhearted, warmhearted, decent, kindly, benign, humane, friendly, generous, loving, nice, tolerant
2. *n* type

king *n* monarch, sovereign, ruler, emperor

knot 1. *n* tangle, snarl, snag, hitch, splice
2. *vb* tie

know *vb* understand, realize, recognize, apprehend, comprehend, see, fathom, grasp, follow, get, penetrate, remember

knowledge *n* fact, information, learning, data, evidence, education, awareness, erudition, experience, wisdom

L

label 1. *n* tag, sticker, ticket, tab, marker, insignia, trademark, logo, service mark, brand, name
2. *vb* mark, ticket, name
3. *vb* stereotype

last 1. *adj* latest, final, ultimate, extreme, concluding, closing, terminal, hindmost, outermost, latter
2. *vb* continue

late 1. *adj* overdue, tardy, belated, delayed, delinquent (antonyms: early, punctual)
2. *adj* new
3. *adj* dead
4. *adv* behind, behindhand, belatedly, tardily

laugh *vb*, *n* giggle, chuckle, snicker, roar, guffaw, snigger, titter, cackle, howl, shriek, smile

layer *n* stratum, tier, sheet, level, film, membrane, coat

lazy *adj* indolent, idle, shiftless, slothful, apathetic, listless (antonym: ambitious)

lead 1. *vb* guide, direct, conduct, usher, steer, take, send, show, funnel, bring (antonym: follow)
2. *vb* direct, manage, supervise, administer, run, preside, oversee, chair, officiate, control, govern, command (antonym: follow)
3. *n* front

learn 1. *vb* ascertain, realize, discover, determine, see, find, find out

2. *vb* memorize, absorb, assimilate, master, digest, study, remember, practice

least *adj* smallest, tiniest, minutest, slightest, minimal, minimum, merest (antonym: best)

leave 1. *vb* depart, exit, embark, withdraw, desert, abandon, vacate, evacuate, forsake, quit, maroon, strand, set out, set off, flee, defect, go, move (antonyms: enter, wait)
2. *vb* disembark, detrain, deplane, land, descend (antonym: enter)
3. *vb* will, bequeath, bestow, hand down, give
4. *n* vacation

legal *adj* lawful, legitimate, permissible, statutory, prescribed, allowable, licit, constitutional, sanctioned, valid, official (antonym: illegal)

legendary *adj* mythical, mythological, fabulous, fabled, apocryphal, traditional, proverbial, imaginary

less 1. *adj* fewer, smaller, diminished, reduced, lower (antonym: more)
2. *prep* minus

lesson *n* class, teaching, drill, exercise, homework, assignment, education

let 1. *vb* allow, permit, authorize, license, tolerate, enable, entitle, qualify, empower, agree (antonym: prevent)
2. *vb* hire

level 1. *adj* flat, smooth, even, flush, parallel, trim, straight

2. *adj* plane, horizontal, flat, low

3. *n* grade, layer, floor

4. *vb* destroy

5. *vb* even, smooth, flatten, grade, plane, straighten

liar *n* fibber, storyteller, deceiver, prevaricator, perjurer, falsifier, equivocator, cheat

lie 1. *n* falsehood, fib, untruth, fiction, story, tale, fabrication, invention, deception, disinformation, misrepresentation, concoction, canard, pretense, dishonesty (antonym: truth)

2. *vb* deceive, fib, prevaricate, falsify, mislead, dissemble, misstate, equivocate, fabricate, invent, pretend

3. *vb* rest, recline, repose, sprawl, loll

life 1. *n* being, animation, vitality, breath, sentience, consciousness, living, existence

2. *n* lifetime, longevity, span, career

3. *n* energy

light¹ 1. *n* radiance, illumination, luminosity, brilliance, brightness, glare, glow, sheen, glimmer, shine, gleam, luster, gloss, glitter, twinkle, sparkle, glint

2. *n* day

3. *n* lamp, lightbulb, bulb, streetlight, lantern, chandelier, flashlight, torch

4. *n* ray, beam, beacon, flash, flare, signal, spark

5. *adj* bright

6. *adj* fair

7. *vb* illuminate, light up, illumine, brighten, lighten

8. *vb* ignite, kindle, strike, fuel, burn

light² 1. *adj* lightweight, underweight, slight, slender, scant, sparse, buoyant, weightless, insubstantial (antonym: heavy)

2. *adj* gentle

3. *adj* easy

4. *vb* descend

like 1. *vb* enjoy, be fond of, care for, relish, fancy, delight in, love, appreciate

2. *adj* alike, same

link 1. *n* connection, association, contact, bond, correlation, attachment, tie, joint, affinity, affiliation, bridge, junction, union

2. *vb* join

list 1. *n* catalog, program, schedule, agenda, outline, menu, roster, inventory, table

2. *vb* itemize, record, catalogue, inventory, register, tabulate, enumerate, specify

3. *vb* slant

listen *vb* hear, hearken, hark, overhear, eavesdrop, attend

live¹ 1. *vb* exist, be, thrive, subsist, breathe, experience

2. *vb* survive, outlive, outlast, persevere, persist, continue (antonym: die)

3. *vb* reside, dwell, stay, abide, inhabit, lodge, room, sojourn, occupy

live² *adj* lively, alive, active

loan 1. *n* credit, advance, mortgage, rental, accommodation, allowance
2. *vb* lend

lonely *adj* lonesome, homesick, solitary, friendless, outcast, alone, sad

long 1. *adj* lengthy, tall, extended, elongated, outstretched, extensive, big (antonym: short)
2. *adj* lengthy, protracted, unending, long-winded, sustained
3. *vb* want

look 1. *vb* watch, glance, observe, witness, view, regard, spy, sight, eye, survey, peek, see, stare, examine
2. *vb* seem, appear, resemble
3. *vb* hunt
4. *n* glance, peek, view, gaze, glimpse, scrutiny, inspection
5. *n* appearance

lose 1. *vb* misplace, mislay, drop, miss, forget (antonym: find)
2. *vb* succumb, fall, fail, surrender (antonym: win)

loud 1. *adj* noisy, resounding, deafening, thunderous, earsplitting, piercing, resonant, strident, shrill, audible, high (antonym: quiet)
2. *adj* boisterous, rowdy, rambunctious, raucous, vociferous, clamorous, obstreperous, stentorian, cacophonous, uproarious, rude
3. *adj* garish, flashy, gaudy, showy, ostentatious, tacky, bright, fancy

love 1. *vb* adore, cherish, admire, worship, idolize, dote on, revere, like, court (antonym: hate)
2. *n* affection, devotion, fondness, passion, tenderness, adoration, attachment, infatuation, kindness, desire, virtue (antonym: hate)
3. *n* lover, beloved, darling, dear, sweetheart, girlfriend, boyfriend, fiancé, fiancée
4. *n* zero (in tennis)

loyalty *n* allegiance, fidelity, faithfulness, devotion, fealty, dependability, dedication, patriotism

luck *n* windfall, godsend, opportunity, break, success, chance

M

magic 1. *adj* enchanted, charmed, magical, mystical, occult, bewitching, entrancing, spellbinding, lucky, mysterious
2. *n* sorcery, witchcraft, wizardry, enchantment, hocus-pocus, voodoo

make 1. *vb* create, make up, manufacture, produce, fashion, model, compose, constitute, forge, strike, build, form, invent
2. *vb* force
3. *vb* earn
4. *n* brand, model, brand name, type

man *n* gentleman, boy, guy, fellow, husband, male, chap, lad, human being, humanity, adult

manufactured *adj* made, machine-made, manmade, mass-produced, synthetic, artificial, human-made

many 1. *adj* numerous, various, countless, manifold, diverse, multiple, innumerable, sundry, myriad, different (antonym: few)
2. *n* abundance

masculine *adj* male, manly, virile, macho, gentlemanly, fatherly (antonym: feminine)

matter 1. *n* substance, material, body, element, constituent, stuff
2. *n* subject
3. *n* business
4. *n* trouble
5. *vb* count, signify, imply, mean

maybe *adv* perhaps, possibly, conceivably, feasibly, perchance, probably

mean 1. *adj* cruel, vicious, malicious, merciless, savage, malignant, ruthless, brutal, low, cold-blooded, inhuman, relentless, pitiless, unkind, violent, revengeful
2. *adj* small-minded, petty, selfish, intolerant, prejudiced, greedy (antonym: tolerant)
3. *adj* middle
4. *n* average
5. *vb* signify, indicate, symbolize, connote, denote, imply, spell, matter, intend, suggest

measure 1. *n* dimension, distance, capacity, weight, volume, mass, amount, number, size, speed
2. *n* rule, gauge, scale, standard, criterion, benchmark, yardstick, touchstone
3. *n* rhythm

4. *vb* weigh, gauge, rule, time

medicine 1. *n* medication, prescription, ⟨...⟩ tablet, capsule, ointment, lo⟨...⟩ injection, shot, vaccine, cur⟨...⟩
2. *n* medic⟨...⟩
profession⟨...⟩

meeting 1⟨...⟩
engage⟨...⟩
tryst, e⟨...⟩
run-in, bru⟨...⟩
2. *n* conference, asse⟨...⟩ gathering, reunion, conven⟨...⟩ council, interview, session, talk
3. *n* introduction
4. *n* junction

melt *vb* dissolve, thaw, liquefy, fuse, evaporate, soften, disappear

member 1. *n* affiliate, constituent, fellow, enrollee, colleague, participant, partner
2. *n* limb

memory *n* recollection, reminiscence, recall, remembrance, déjà vu

mention 1. *vb* refer to, touch on, infer, allude, state, name, specify, say, suggest, broach
2. *n* remark

messy *adj* untidy, disorderly, sloppy, slovenly, disheveled, bedraggled, unkempt, dirty (antonym: neat)

method *n* approach, procedure, process, technique, system, routine, manner, way, plan

middle 1. *n* center, core, midpoint, hub, nucleus, focus, midst, interior, inside, soul, depth, essence

2. *adj* central, inner, interior, median, mean, midmost, intermediate, inside, average

miracle *n* wonder, marvel, phenomenon, rarity, oddity, portent

mischievous *adj* naughty, disobedient, unruly, wayward, spoiled, ill-behaved, impish, elfish, elfin, rude, rebellious, bad (antonym: good)

misery *n* suffering, agony, anguish, distress, grief, pain, torment, torture, heartache, hardship, sorrow

mistake 1. *n* error, slip, blunder, oversight, faux pas, inaccuracy, fallacy, miscalculation, fault, defect, misunderstanding

2. *vb* misunderstand

misunderstand *vb* misinterpret, misjudge, misconstrue, mistake, err

mix 1. *vb* combine, blend, merge, mingle, compound, consolidate, stir, whip, beat, knead, roll, churn, jumble, scramble, shuffle, join

2. *vb* associate, mingle, intermingle, socialize, fraternize, consort, join

3. *n* assortment

model 1. *n* paragon, ideal, archetype, exemplar, paradigm, nonpareil, standard, prototype, original, example

2. *n* miniature, representation, reduction, mock-up, copy, duplicate

3. *n* make, pattern

4. *n* subject, sitter, fashion model, poser, mannequin

5. *vb* make

6. *vb* pose, sit, show

7. *adj* classic, outstanding, first-rate, excellent, authoritative, typical, archetypal, definitive, perfect

modern *adj* contemporary, current, up-to-date, stylish, recent, modernistic, newfangled, space-age, state-of-the-art, latter-day, new

moment 1. *n* instant, point, minute, second, twinkling, wink, jiffy, flash, trice, time, period

2. *n* importance

money *n* cash, currency, coin, revenue, capital, specie, wealth, property

mood *n* humor, morale, temper, temperament, disposition, spirits, vein, state, setting

more 1. *adj* additional, extra, added, further, supplementary, another, new (antonym: less)

2. *adv* additionally, furthermore, still, yet, better, preferably, sooner, rather

3. *n* increase, supplement, extra, surplus

most 1. *adj* maximum, utmost, greatest

2. *n* majority, maximum, bulk, preponderance

3. *adv* very, best

move 1. *vb* shift, remove, budge,

dislodge, carry, push
2. *vb* transfer, relocate, migrate, emigrate, immigrate, leave, go, travel
3. *vb* affect
4. *vb* suggest

much 1. *adv* greatly, enormously, extremely, dearly, very, far
2. *adj* enough, abundant
3. *n* abundance

murder 1. *n* homicide, manslaughter, assassination, bloodshed, massacre, slaughter, slaying, carnage, annihilation, crime
2. *vb* kill

mysterious *adj* puzzling, enigmatic, perplexing, baffling, inexplicable, uncanny, mystic, mystical, magic, strange, obscure

myth *n* legend, fable, epic, lore, folklore, tradition, mythology, story, superstition

N

naive *adj* unsophisticated, inexperienced, simple, innocent, artless, ingenuous, trusting, green, gullible, credulous, unaware, amateur, harmless

native 1. *adj* indigenous, aboriginal, endemic, original, domestic, local, homegrown, natural
2. *n* citizen

natural 1. *adj* organic, pure, unprocessed, raw, uncooked, plain, normal
2. *adj* inborn, inherent, instinctive,

innate, hereditary, inherited, congenital, genetic, intrinsic, native

nausea *n* indigestion, queasiness, vomiting, sickness, qualm, illness

near 1. *adj* close, nearby, immediate, intimate, imminent, local, adjacent, about, approximate
2. *adj* future
3. *prep* beside
4. *vb* approach

neat *adj* tidy, trim, orderly, organized, shipshape, precise, spruce, clean, prim, legible (antonym: messy)

necessary *adj* essential, indispensable, basic, required, requisite, fundamental, mandatory, compulsory, obligatory, imperative, important

need 1. *vb* require, lack, want
2. *vb* must, should, ought, have
3. *n* necessity, reason
4. *n* hardship, poverty

negotiate *vb* mediate, moderate, bargain, referee, confer, transact, haggle, parley, intercede, arbitrate, decide

neighborhood *n* community, block, vicinity, quarter, precinct, ward, borough, place, zone

nervous *adj* restless, fidgety, shaky, edgy, uptight, skittish, self-conscious, jittery, jumpy,

high-strung *adj* afraid, anxious, cowardly

new 1. *adj* fresh, original, recent, late, latest, novel, brand-new, trendy, up-to-date, unused, unspoiled, pristine, virgin, untouched, modern (antonym: old)

2. *adj* more

nice 1. *adj* agreeable, delightful, fantastic, good, great, pleasant

2. *adj* good-natured, charming, pleasant, agreeable, affable, good-humored, thoughtful, polite, friendly, kind

3. *adj* careful

noble 1. *adj* royal, aristocratic, highborn, patrician, titled, blue-blooded, princely, kingly, regal, imperial, elite

2. *adj* worthy, generous, magnanimous, courtly, chivalrous, chivalric, grand, good

3. *n* nobleman, noblewoman, aristocrat, peer, lord, lady

noise *n* sound, din, uproar, clamor, racket, hubbub, tumult, commotion, pandemonium, hullabaloo, peal, bang, cry, peep

normal *adj* typical, average, natural, standard, conventional, common, usual

notice 1. *vb* observe, note, perceive, discover, look, see

2. *n* attention, observation, regard, heed, note, publicity, warning

3. *n* advertisement, announcement, reminder

now *adv* immediately, straightaway, directly, right away, instantly, quickly, soon

number 1. *n* numeral, figure, digit, cipher, integer, fraction

2. *n* amount, quantity, batch, lot, bunch, bundle, group, assortment

3. *n* act

O

obey *vb* comply, mind, follow, heed, behave, adhere, observe, meet (antonym: disobey)

object 1. *vb* protest, disagree, dissent, oppose, dispute, disapprove, frown, argue, complain, contradict (antonym: agree)

2. *n* thing, article, item, gadget, device

3. *n* objective, purpose, aim, goal, sake, target, intention, intent, ambition

obvious *adj* clear, evident, apparent, transparent, noticeable, overt, glaring, blatant, gross, conspicuous, prominent, palpable, pronounced, marked, distinct, patent, bald, easy, plain (antonym: obscure)

offer 1. *vb* propose, present, tender, bid, proffer, extend, suggest, quote, give, sell

2. *n* suggestion, invitation

official 1. *adj* authentic, authorized, legitimate, approved, licensed, valid, formal, real, correct

2. *n* leader, administrator, executive, bureaucrat, civil servant, public servant, boss, judge

often *adv* frequently, repeatedly, oftentimes, recurrently, regularly, usually (antonym: seldom)

old 1. *adj* elderly, aged, venerable, mature, senior, hoary, seasoned (antonym: young)

2. *adj* ancient, old-fashioned, antique, archaic, antiquated, obsolete, outdated (antonym: new)

3. *adj* worn, used, rundown, worn-out, secondhand, decrepit, shabby, ragged

only 1. *adv* just, barely, hardly, scarcely, merely, simply, exclusively

2. *adj* single, sole, solitary, unique, one, lone

open 1. *adj* ajar, uncovered, unfastened, unlocked, accessible, unobstructed, unsealed

2. *adj* spacious, deserted, clear, empty

3. *vb* unfasten, undo, unbolt, untie, free, clear, separate

4. *vb* start

operate *vb* function, perform, run, drive, act, work, use

opponent *n* rival, competitor, opposition, challenger, antagonist, adversary, foe, competition, contestant, enemy (antonym: friend)

opportunity *n* chance, occasion, excuse, opening, situation, luck

opposite 1. *adj* opposing, contradictory, contrary, conflicting, inverse, converse, reverse, contrasting, antithetical, counter, different

2. *adj* facing, opposed, fronting, confronting

3. *n* reverse, contrary, converse, antithesis, inverse

4. *prep* facing, across from, against, opposed to, versus

optimistic *adj* hopeful, confident, cheerful, sanguine, expectant, bullish, idealistic, certain (antonym: pessimistic)

order 1. *vb* command, direct, instruct, decree, bid, dictate, impose, prescribe, ordain, mandate, ask, tell, insist, force

2. *vb* arrange, straighten

3. *n* arrangement, formation, organization, layout, disposition, alignment, placement, sequence, succession, system, plan

4. *n* decree, command, commandment, demand, ultimatum, direction, directive, charge, mandate, edict, behest, writ

5. *n* religion

organization 1. *n* association, corporation, institution, foundation, society, club, fraternity, sorority, business, union, group

2. *n* order

outside 1. *n* exterior, surface, façade

2. *adj* exterior, external, outer, outermost, outward, outdoor, alfresco

3. *adv* outdoors, out-of-doors, out, alfresco

own 1. *vb* possess, hold, have, retain, maintain, enjoy, occupy, keep

2. *vb* admit

3. *adj* private

P

page 1. *n* sheet, leaf, folio
2. *n* intern, servant
3. *vb* call

pain 1. *n* suffering, discomfort, ache, pang, soreness, twinge, stitch, spasm, cramp, sting
2. *n* misery
3. *n* nuisance

pair 1. *n* couple, duo, twosome, twins, brace (of animals), yoke (of oxen), span (of horses), team
2. *vb* join

paper 1. *n* stationery, notepaper, writing paper, newsprint, crepe paper, tissue, wax paper, tar paper, parchment, vellum
2. *n* document, report
3. *n* newspaper, magazine, journal, periodical, tabloid, gazette, daily, weekly

parade 1. *n* procession, march, demonstration, cavalcade, motorcade
2. *vb* walk, strut
3. *vb* advertise

parallel 1. *adj* equidistant, collateral, aligned, even, alongside, abreast, level
2. *adj* alike
3. *n* duplicate, similarity
4. *vb* compare

part 1. *n* piece, section, portion, segment, fragment, fraction, share, element, facet, aspect, component, ingredient, content, bit, block, division (antonym: total)
2. *n* role, function
3. *vb* divide, separate

partner 1. *n* associate, co-worker, confederate, accomplice, accessory, sidekick, helper
2. *n* friend
3. *n* love, spouse

party 1. *n* celebration, festivity, gathering, reception, soiree, fete, occasion, gala, function, revelry, jubilee, merrymaking, feast
2. *n* faction, bloc, league, lobby, junta, cabal, organization, group
3. *n* participant, litigant, principal, member, contestant
4. *vb* celebrate

past 1. *adj* former, preceding, foregoing, prior, previous, antecedent, old
2. *adj* finished, over, ended, through, done
3. *n* history, antiquity, yesterday, yesteryear, yore
4. *prep* beyond, through, behind, over, after

path *n* pathway, footpath, trail, track, lane, walk, walkway, runway, shortcut, road, course

patient 1. *adj* understanding, forbearing, mild-tempered, long-suffering, tolerant, calm, passive
2. *adj* persistent, perservering, steadfast, assiduous, diligent
3. *n* subject, victim, sufferer, convalescent, invalid, outpatient, inpatient

patriotic *adj* loyal, zealous, nationalistic, chauvinistic, faithful

pattern 1. *n* design, motif, configuration, structure, plan
2. *n* model, blueprint, template, diagram, guide, sketch
3. *vb* form

pay 1. *vb* compensate, recompense, spend, reward, tip, remunerate, settle, disburse, expend, atone, expiate, give, earn, refund
2. *n* wage

peace *n* harmony, concord, repose, amity, reconciliation, agreement, calm, truce

pen 1. *n* corral, fold, pound, paddock, enclosure, coop, cage, sty, stall, kennel, barn, field, jail
2. *n* ballpoint, marker, fountain pen, quill, nib
3. *vb* write

people 1. *n* citizenry, populace, public, population, society, civilization, community, folk, hoi polloi, bourgeoisie, human being, humanity, citizen
2. *n* family

perfect 1. *adj* ideal, flawless, faultless, impeccable, unblemished, immaculate, exquisite, exemplary, model, correct, infallible
2. *adj* pure, sheer, outright, complete
3. *vb* polish, hone, amend, fix, correct

period 1. *n* interval, term, span, spell, duration, extent, stretch, streak, cycle, bout, season, phase, stage, time, shift, watch, tour, stint, round, moment
2. *n* age, eon, era, epoch, date

permanent *adj* durable, lasting, enduring, abiding, perennial, persistent, indelible, continual, eternal, stationary (antonym: temporary)

permission *n* consent, authorization, authority, approval, license, sanction, support

personality 1. *n* character, disposition, temperament, temper, nature, identity
2. *n* charisma, charm, presence, allure, magnetism, bearing, attraction
3. *n* celebrity

perspective *n* point of view, viewpoint, standpoint, orientation, direction, angle, position, attitude, side, view

persuade *vb* convince, satisfy, influence, induce, dispose, coax, sway, get, wheedle, cajole, entice, prevail, snow, urge, tempt (antonym: discourage)

pessimistic *adj* cynical, negative, glum, sullen, morose, fatalistic, bleak, sad (antonym: optimistic)

physical *adj* bodily, corporal, corporeal, fleshly, real

picture 1. *n* portrait, image, drawing, painting, illustration, representation, diagram, sketch, cartoon, poster, work, plate, print, description, photograph, X ray
2. *n* movie
3. *vb* imagine
4. *vb* draw

pile 1. *n* heap, stack, mound, hill, lump, wad, clump, mass, nugget, bulk, assortment
2. *n* post
3. *vb* heap, stack, gather

pioneer 1. *n* settler, homesteader, backwoodsman, frontiersman, immigrant, colonist, colonizer
2. *n* creator
3. *adj* early

pirate 1. *n* buccaneer, privateer, freebooter, corsair, plunderer, marauder, criminal, vandal
2. *vb* steal

pity 1. *n* sympathy, compassion, empathy, mercy, forbearance, ruth, clemency, condolence, commiseration, kindness, comfort
2. *n* disaster
3. *vb* sympathize, commiserate, comfort

place 1. *n* location, position, situation, locale, site, spot, locality, region, vicinity, space, zone
2. *n* house
3. *n* profession
4. *vb* locate, situate, assign, store, put
5. *vb* arrange

plain 1. *adj* simple, uncomplicated, unadorned, unvarnished, frugal, severe, austere, stark, common, humble, natural, naked (antonym: complicated)
2. *adj* unattractive, homely, drab, unlovely, ugly (antonym: pretty)
3. *adj* obvious, straightforward
4. *n* prairie, range, grassland, savanna, heath, moor, tundra, downs, field, plateau

plan 1. *n* design, project, plot, schematic, outline, map, table
2. *n* aim, intent, goal, purpose, strategy, scheme, plot, conspiracy, program, policy, platform, plank, provision, method, recipe
3. *vb* plot, scheme, conspire, contrive, connive, chart, map, outline, arrange, prepare, intend

planet *n* heavenly body, celestial body, satellite, earth, space

plant 1. *n* shrub, weed, grass, bush, vegetation, flora, foliage, organism, flower, tree, herb, vegetable, fruit
2. *n* factory
3. *vb* seed, sow, pot, transplant, propagate, set, broadcast, scatter, grow
4. *vb* put

plateau 1. *n* tableland, table, mesa, steppe, upland, highland, plain
2. *n* grade

play 1. *vb* frisk, sport, disport, romp, frolic, gambol, recreate
2. *vb* compete
3. *vb* perform, finger, bow, strum, practice, blow
4. *vb* act
5. *vb* run, show, present, air, broadcast
6. *n* recreation, horseplay, clowning, pleasure, entertainment
7. *n* drama, dramatization, skit, pageant, tragedy, melodrama, comedy, farce, musical, mystery, program, movie

8. *n* movement

please *vb* delight, gratify, gladden, content, hearten, satisfy, entertain, pamper

poison 1. *n* venom, toxin, bane, infection, virus, germ
2. *vb* kill

polite *adj* courteous, well-mannered, civil, chivalrous, gracious, friendly, thoughtful, nice, prim (antonym: rude)

poor 1. *adj* needy, penniless, destitute, broke, impoverished, deprived, indigent, poverty-stricken (antonym: rich)
2. *adj* pitiful, sorry, paltry, inferior, shoddy, deficient, pedestrian, tawdry, unsatisfactory, inadequate, worthless, wretched, abject, lame

possession 1. *n* ownership, custody, title, proprietorship, receipt, control, rule
2. *n* property, acquisition
3. *n* colony

possible *adj* plausible, conceivable, believable, credible, feasible, potential, reasonable, imaginable, practicable, viable, likely

poverty *n* destitution, want, need, penury, indigence, privation, impoverishment, hardship

practical 1. *adj* matter-of-fact, down-to-earth, realistic, reasonable, rational, sensible, unsentimental, able (antonym: impractical)
2. *adj* useful, efficient
3. *adj* virtual

practice 1. *vb* rehearse, drill, train, study, learn
2. *vb* use
3. *n* rehearsal, repetition, preparation, discipline
4. *n* habit

praise 1. *n* applause, acclaim, compliment, approval, adulation, acclamation, kudos, congratulations, flattery, respect
2. *vb* commend, extol, acclaim, laud, compliment, honor, decorate, congratulate, toast, rave, celebrate, clap, flatter, worship

predict *vb* forecast, foretell, prophesy, prognosticate, project, divine, tell, foresee, augur, portend, presage, anticipate

prefer *vb* favor, endorse, advocate, choose, like, want

prejudice *n* intolerance, bigotry, bias, partiality, predisposition, predilection, favoritism, discrimination, racism, sexism, chauvinism, ageism, hatred

prepare *vb* develop, provide, ready, plan, adapt, prime, process, refine, arrange, cook, make, invent

pretend *vb* feign, affect, simulate, profess, act, assume, imagine, lie, fake

pretty *adj* lovely, handsome, attractive, good-looking, fair, becoming, comely, striking, beautiful, cute (antonym: ugly, plain)

prevent *vb* avert, hinder, forestall, check, restrain, thwart, foil, frustrate, deter, inhibit, stunt, hobble, leash, stop, block, discourage, contain (antonym: let)

prey 1. *n* quarry, victim, target
2. *vb* eat
3. *vb* cheat

price *n* charge, expense, cost, fare, payment, amount, fee, consideration, outlay, worth, bill

pride 1. *n* self-respect, self-esteem, dignity, self-confidence, respect
2. *n* vanity, conceit, arrogance, vainglory, egotism, hubris, narcissism, haughtiness
3. *n* pleasure

primitive 1. *adj* basic
2. *adj* early
3. *adj* uncivilized, simple, crude, rough, rustic, unsophisticated, untamed, aboriginal, pristine

print 1. *vb* publish, issue, reprint, write
2. *vb* imprint, impress, engrave, stamp, emboss, inscribe .
3. *n* etching, engraving, woodcut, lithograph, photocopy, photograph, picture
4. *n* impression, imprint, indentation, fingerprint, footprint, track
5. *n* text, printing, type, typescript, writing

prisoner *n* captive, inmate, detainee, internee, slave, hostage

private 1. *adj* secluded, isolated, remote, withdrawn, insular, quarantined
2. *adj* personal, individual, intimate, own (antonym: public)

3. *adj* exclusive, restricted, reserved, special (antonym: public)
4. *adj* secret

probably *adv* presumably, apparently, plausibly, seemingly, maybe

problem 1. *n* mystery, puzzle, riddle, dilemma, enigma, ambiguity, conundrum, contradiction, question
2. *n* trouble

profession *n* occupation, employment, appointment, vocation, avocation, calling, career, livelihood, post, position, situation, place, craft, trade, job, field, business, specialty

program 1. *n* performance, concert, recital, show, production, broadcast, telecast, presentation, series, play, movie, entertainment
2. *n* list
3. *n* plan, course

progress 1. *n* improvement, progression, headway, advance, advancement, momentum, movement, growth, success
2. *vb* go

promise 1. *n* oath, vow, word, pledge, assurance, commitment, covenant, guarantee
2. *vb* swear, pledge, vow, assure, warrant, guarantee

proof *n* evidence, testimony, verification, certification, documentation, data, corroboration, confirmation, substantiation, authentication

property 1. *n* possessions,

belongings, effects, goods, assets, holdings, capital, things, stuff, wealth, acquisition
2. *n* land, lot, estate, yard, grounds, premises, plot, tract
3. *n* quality

protect 1. *vb* defend, guard, shield, safeguard, fortify, watch, mind, tend, save, patrol (antonym: attack)
2. *vb* shelter, cover, cushion, pad

protest 1. *n* demonstration, strike, sit-in, teach-in, rally, complaint
2. *vb* demonstrate, picket, strike, walk out, complain, object
3. *vb* complain, object, argue

proud 1. *adj* egotistic, conceited, vain, arrogant, egocentric, haughty, smug, superior, pretentious, pompous (antonym: humble)
2. *adj* grand
3. *adj* happy

pull 1. *vb* tow, drag, haul, draw, tug, yank, jerk, pluck, attract, bring, tighten, strain, extract (antonym: push)
2. *vb* sprain, strain, hurt
3. *n* tug, yank, drag, jerk, wrench, attraction

punctual *adj* timely, prompt, precise, expeditious, punctilious (antonym: late)

punish *vb* discipline, penalize, sentence, correct, fine, abuse, hurt, hit, scold, whip

punishment *n* penalty, sentence, penance, deserts, retribution,

consequence, discipline, abuse

push 1. *vb* press, shove, impel, thrust, jostle, nudge, elbow, shoulder, slide, prod, poke, ram, jam, wedge, move, force (antonym: pull)
2. *vb* urge
3. *n* blow, impulse

put *vb* set, lay, park, deposit, plant, position, implant, install, insert, place

Q

quality *n* property, characteristic, character, trait, attribute, air, atmosphere, texture, tone, class, feeling

question 1. *n* query, inquiry, interrogation, interrogative, problem (antonym: answer)
2. *n* doubt
3. *n* subject
4. *vb* ask

quickly *adv* speedily, hastily, hurriedly, fast, rapidly, expeditiously, instantaneously, promptly, headlong, now, soon

quiet 1. *adj* silent, still, hushed, noiseless, soundless, inaudible, mute, mum, speechless, low (antonym: loud)
2. *n* calm
3. *vb* hush, silence, soften, mute, muffle, stifle, muzzle, gag

quote 1. *vb* cite, repeat, parrot, paraphrase, recite, declaim, render, mention, say, tell

2. *n* estimate

R

race 1. *n* run, dash, sprint, relay, marathon, footrace, horse race, steeplechase, derby, game
2. *n* type
3. *n* humanity
4. *vb* run, hurry

rain 1. *n* precipitation, shower, downpour, drizzle, cloudburst, torrent, storm
2. *vb* pour, drizzle, sprinkle, shower, teem, precipitate

range 1. *n* extent, scope, spread, reach, compass, sweep, spectrum, assortment, space, horizon
2. *n* plain
3. *vb* wander
4. *vb* spread

rare *adj* uncommon, scarce, infrequent, occasional, special, valuable

read 1. *vb* peruse, skim, scan, browse, study
2. *vb* comprehend, decipher, decode, perceive
3. *vb* indicate, register, record, show

ready 1. *adj* prepared, set, qualified, ripe, equipped, available
2. *adj* willing, disposed, predisposed, eager, likely
3. *vb* prepare

real 1. *adj* actual, material, tangible, substantive, concrete, objective, solid, true, palpable, physical

(antonym: imaginary)
2. *adj* actual, genuine, authentic, bona fide, veritable, literal, legitimate, pure, natural (antonym: fake)

really 1. *adv* actually, genuinely, literally, indeed, veritably, certainly
2. *adv* very

reason 1. *n* purpose, cause, motive, explanation, call, grounds, need, rationale, necessity, incentive, justification
2. *n* logic, reasoning, thinking, induction, deduction, analysis, wisdom
3. *n* sanity, mental health, lucidity, saneness
4. *vb* think, infer

rebel 1. *vb* revolt, mutiny, resist, defy, face, dare
2. *n* revolutionary, insurgent, mutineer, subversive, dissident, freedom fighter, traitor, turncoat, extremist

receive 1. *vb* accept, admit, take, inherit, greet, get (antonyms: give, refuse)
2. *vb* welcome, entertain

recently *adv* lately, newly, just, latterly

reflect 1. *vb* echo, mirror, ricochet, rebound, bounce
2. *vb* consider, meditate

refund 1. *vb* reimburse, repay, remit, compensate, pay
2. *n* reimbursement, repayment, compensation, rebate

refuse 1. *vb* deny, reject, decline,

dismiss, disapprove, spurn,
repudiate, rebuff, snub, scorn,
flout, deprive, repel
2. *n* trash

regret 1. *vb* repent, apologize,
bewail, bemoan, lament, deplore,
rue, grieve
2. *n* compunction, repentance,
disappointment, sorrow, shame

regularly *adv* constantly, invariably,
always, ever, continually,
habitually, routinely, religiously,
naturally, typically, often, usually,
forever

relationship *n* relation, kinship,
affinity, rapport, compatibility,
link, friendship

relevant *adj* pertinent, germane,
apposite, applicable, apropos,
related, relative, fit

reliable *adj* dependable,
trustworthy, responsible,
reputable, unimpeachable, solid,
conscientious, sure, surefire,
faithful, able, indisputable

religion 1. *n* faith, mythology,
theology, religiosity, spirituality,
orthodoxy, belief, philosophy
2. *n* denomination, sect, order,
cult

reluctant *adj* hesitant, unwilling,
grudging, disinclined, loath,
averse, diffident, squeamish

remember *vb* recall, recollect,
reminisce, remind, recognize,
commemorate, memorialize,
know, learn (antonym: forget)

repair 1. *n* adjustment,
improvement, renovation,
restoration, patch, plug, mend,
service, servicing, correction
2. *vb* fix

repeat 1. *vb* redo, replicate,
duplicate, reduplicate, reproduce
2. *vb* recur, reoccur
3. *vb* reiterate, restate, recapitulate,
echo, rehearse, rehash, recount,
quote

report 1. *n* essay, paper,
composition, theme, treatise,
thesis, dissertation, article,
announcement, speech, story,
study
2. *n* bang
3. *vb* tell

reproduce 1. *vb* copy, duplicate,
photocopy, clone, imitate
2. *vb* procreate, breed, propagate,
multiply, proliferate, generate,
beget, spawn, hatch

resemble *vb* look like, take after,
match, approximate, favor,
correspond

respect 1. *n* admiration, honor,
reverence, dignity, homage,
esteem, regard, estimation,
deference, courtesy, awe, wonder,
prestige, pride
2. *vb* esteem, admire, revere, value,
prize, cherish, appreciate
3. *vb* keep

rest 1. *vb* relax, repose, unwind,
recuperate, lounge, loaf, laze, idle,
sleep, lie
2. *vb* depend
3. *n* relaxation, repose, ease, sleep,
break, vacation

4. *n* remainder

return 1. *vb* come back, go back, revisit, recur, reoccur, resurface, reappear, rebound, renew
2. *n* arrival, homecoming, reappearance, recurrence, reoccurrence, resurgence
3. *n* recovery, restoration, restitution, reimbursement, repayment
4. *n* wage

revenge 1. *n* vengeance, retaliation, repayment, compensation, satisfaction, vindication
2. *vb* avenge, retaliate, repay, requite, vindicate

revolution 1. *n* rebellion, revolt, insurrection, uprising, coup, coup d'état, insurgence, treason, disturbance
2. *n* change
3. *n* circle

rich 1. *adj* wealthy, affluent, prosperous, well-to-do, moneyed, well-off, comfortable, posh, successful (antonym: poor)
2. *adj* opulent, resplendent, ornate, lavish, lush, luxurious, profuse, grand, fashionable, expensive, fancy
3. *adj* sweet, sugary, creamy, buttery, fattening, luscious, succulent, cloying, saccharine, honeyed, delicious
4. *n* aristocracy

right 1. *n* power, privilege, prerogative, authority, license, freedom
2. *adj* correct, fit, fair (antonym: wrong)
3. *adv* correctly
4. *adv* soon
5. *adv* precisely

road *n* street, avenue, boulevard, thoroughfare, artery, roadway, lane, alley, highway, path

rough 1. *adj* coarse, uneven, rugged, irregular, bumpy, jagged, crumpled, rumpled, harsh, scratchy, hoarse
2. *adj* choppy, raging, ruffled, wild, stormy
3. *adj* rude, primitive
4. *adj* hard
5. *adj* approximate

rude *adj* impolite, insolent, discourteous, ungracious, impertinent, impudent, fresh, uncouth, crude, coarse, crass, bold, brash, presumptuous, audacious, sassy, forward, surly, pert, flip, disrespectful, irreverent, cheeky, abrupt, cross, thoughtless (antonym: polite)

rule 1. *n* law, regulation, custom, principle, axiom, guideline, code, precept, canon, ultimatum, act, habit
2. *n* command, control, authority, mastery, sway, sovereignty, charge, government, jurisdiction, dominion, leadership
3. *n* measure
4. *vb* govern
5. *vb* decide

ruler *n* potentate, prince, lord, governor, leader, president, premier, prime minister, king, queen, emperor, empress, dictator

rumor *n* gossip, hearsay, scandal, talk

run 1. *vb* jog, trot, dash, sprint, bolt, dart, streak, gallop, lope, canter, hurry, race
2. *vb* escape, leave
3. *vb* lead
4. *vb* operate
5. *vb* play
6. *vb* flow
7. *n* race

S

sad *adj* unhappy, miserable, depressed, gloomy, dismal, melancholy, blue, downhearted, downcast, dejected, despondent, doleful, forlorn, moody, down, low, bad, glum, lonely, pitiful, sorry, thoughtful, pessimistic (antonym: happy)

safe 1. *adj* secure, protected, harmless, snug, guarded, impregnable, invulnerable, immune, invincible (antonym: dangerous)
2. *n* vault, strongbox, chest, coffer, treasury, safe-deposit box, cash register

sale 1. *n* deal, transaction, purchase, marketing, auction, trade
2. *n* bargain, deal, clearance, closeout, discount

same *adj* identical, equal, equivalent, corresponding, matching, uniform, consistent, like, alike (antonym: different)

sarcastic *adj* scornful, snide, ironic, ironical, satiric, satirical, sardonic, caustic, derisive

satisfy 1. *vb* appease, slake, quench, sate, satiate, please, relieve, pacify
2. *vb* persuade
3. *vb* suffice, serve, do, fulfill, answer

save 1. *vb* keep, preserve, conserve, maintain, hoard, stockpile, stash, gather (antonyms: discard, abolish, waste)
2. *vb* rescue, deliver, salvage, spare, free, protect
3. *vb* bank
4. *prep* but

say *vb* state, speak, remark, exclaim, phrase, verbalize, express, signify, air, vent, dictate, talk, tell, pronounce, reveal

scary *adj* frightening, frightful, dreadful, terrifying, terrible, horrifying, unnerving, appalling, fearful, awesome

secret 1. *adj* hidden, arcane, cryptic, esoteric, mysterious, anonymous
2. *adj* clandestine, confidential, classified, top secret, private, covert, undercover, surreptitious, underground, sly
3. *n* mystery, confidence, intrigue, problem

see 1. *vb* behold, discern, observe, perceive, notice, glimpse, spot, remark, look
2. *vb* know, learn
3. *vb* imagine

sell *vb* carry, stock, retail, handle,

trade (in), market, peddle, vend, barter, hawk, offer

send 1. *vb* dispatch, transmit, mail, post, e-mail, forward, convey, ship, transfer, export, spread, broadcast
2. *vb* lead
3. *vb* throw

sense 1. *n* sensation, function, capability, feeling, ability
2. *n* wisdom
3. *n* meaning

serious 1. *adj* solemn, grave, somber, earnest, sedate, sober, heavy, important, profound, dignified
2. *adj* sincere

setting *n* environment, surroundings, framework, background, context, backdrop, scenery, climate, ambiance, mood, medium, milieu

shake 1. *vb* vibrate, tremble, shudder, shiver, quiver, quake, quaver, flutter, wobble, wag, waggle, pulsate, throb, jar, tingle
2. *vb* spread
3. *n* vibration

shame 1. *n* disgrace, dishonor, discredit, humiliation, remorse, regret, contrition, embarrassment, chagrin, guilt
2. *vb* humiliate, dishonor, disgrace, debase, abase, demean, discredit, embarrass

share 1. *n* division, percentage, allowance, allotment, stake, quota, ration, proportion, fraction, percent, ratio, part, interest
2. *vb* distribute, apportion, split

(up), deal out, ration, mete out, divide, budget

sharp 1. *adj* keen, acute, honed, pointed, pointy, sharp-edged, knife-edged
2. *adj* smart
3. *adj* acute, abrupt, rapid, sudden
4. *adj* steep
5. *adj* severe, biting, caustic, bitter, harsh, cutting, fierce, brutal, oppressive
6. *adj* spicy, sour
7. *adj* smelly
8. *adj* fashionable

shine 1. *vb* radiate, beam, sparkle, gleam, glow, shimmer, glisten, twinkle
2. *vb* polish, burnish, buff, wax, scour, clean, finish
3. *n* light

shock 1. *vb* astound, appall, dismay, devastate, overwhelm, stun, electrify, stagger, awe, horrify, surprise, scare
2. *n* blow, vibration
3. *n* earthquake
4. *n* blow, upset, jolt, ordeal, trauma, surprise
5. *n* lock

short 1. *adj* slight, low, undersized, skimpy, brief, small (antonym: long)
2. *adj* brief, concise, compact, succinct, abbreviated, terse, laconic, abridged, fleeting, transient, short-lived, fast, temporary
3. *adj* abrupt

4. *adj* inadequate

show 1. *vb* display, exhibit, present, manifest, produce, reveal, advertise, model
2. *vb* lead
3. *vb* explain, verify
4. *n* spectacle, display, play, movie, program

shy *adj* bashful, timid, meek, retiring, diffident, reserved, demure, deferential, timorous, tentative, humble

sick 1. *adj* ill, ailing, sickly, unwell, unhealthy, nauseous, nauseated, queasy, infirm, indisposed, funny, weak (antonym: healthy)
2. *adj* gruesome

sign 1. *n* symbol, signal, token, omen, clue, index, indication, manifestation, symptom, gesture, expression, track, warning
2. *vb* autograph, inscribe, endorse, countersign, initial, write

sincere *adj* genuine, honest, heartfelt, wholehearted, true, trustworthy, serious, straight, straightforward

sink 1. *vb* submerge, submerse, swamp, engulf, immerse, duck, dunk, dip, descend, fall, flood
2. *n* washbasin, basin, lavatory, washstand, bowl

size *n* magnitude, mass, volume, bulk, quantity, proportion, capacity

slavery *n* bondage, servitude, enslavement, serfdom, subjugation, vassalage (antonym: freedom)

slow 1. *adj* leisurely, gradual, sluggish, deliberate, moderate, torpid (antonym: fast)
2. *adj* dilatory, lackadaisical, passive, lazy, listless
3. *adj* dull, stupid

small 1. *adj* little, tiny, miniature, minute, diminutive, Lilliputian, compact, trivial (antonym: big)
2. *adj* scanty, meager, slight, spare, skimpy, stingy, paltry, inadequate

smart 1. *adj* intelligent, clever, bright, wise, learned, brilliant, keen, acute, quick, alert, apt, astute, perceptive, insightful, discerning, incisive, canny, shrewd, precocious, educated, profound (antonyms: foolish, stupid)
2. *adj* fashionable
3. *vb* hurt

smell 1. *n* scent, odor, aroma, fragrance, perfume, incense, bouquet, stench
2. *vb, n* sniff, whiff, scent, sense
3. *vb, n* stink, reek

sneak 1. *vb* creep, slink, prowl, skulk, steal, tiptoe, lurk
2. *n* rascal

soldier *n* fighter, warrior, volunteer, conscript, draftee, recruit, cadet, veteran, officer, serviceman, servicewoman, combatant, mercenary, soldier of fortune, gladiator, army, troop

solve *vb* figure out, puzzle out, resolve, decode, decipher, answer, do, work (out), unravel, unscramble, explain

soon *adv* presently, shortly, forthwith, momentarily, anon, quickly, now

sorry 1. *adj* sorrowful, repentant, apologetic, contrite, penitent, remorseful, sad
2. *adj* forlorn, wretched, depressing, sad, pitiful
3. *adj* poor

source 1. *n* origin, derivation, birthplace, cradle, fountain, fountainhead, font, fount, well, wellspring
2. *n* beginning, cause

space 1. *n* universe, cosmos, heavens, outer space, infinity, void, air
2. *n* room, area, scope, range, expanse, territory, elbowroom

special 1. *adj* distinct, particular, specific, especial, distinctive, respective, proper, certain, unique
2. *adj* select, choice, extraordinary, exceptional, unusual, peculiar, remarkable, noteworthy, phenomenal, outstanding, rare, striking, strange

speech 1. *n* voice, communication, discourse, intercourse, utterance, articulation, diction, locution, enunciation, expression, talk, language, remark, accent, dialect
2. *n* lecture, talk, sermon, address, report, oration

speed 1. *n* velocity, acceleration, swiftness, pace, rate, tempo, rapidity, celerity, dispatch, hurry
2. *vb* hurry

spot 1. *n* speck, dot, mark, taint, stain, blot, blemish, blotch, smudge
2. *n* place
3. *n* trouble
4. *vb* find, see

spread 1. *vb* distribute, disseminate, disperse, circulate, strew, shake, sprinkle, scatter, send, broadcast
2. *vb* extend, stretch, range, unfold, expand, widen, gape, yawn
3. *vb* cover
4. *vb* rub
5. *n* growth
6. *n* range
7. *n* farm
8. *n* feast
9. *n* flow

spying *n* espionage, surveillance, intelligence, counterespionage, counterintelligence

stare *vb* gaze, peer, gape, ogle, gawk, look

start 1. *vb* begin, commence, initiate, cause, activate, launch, originate, stem, inaugurate, introduce, innovate, open, trigger, touch off, spark, continue (antonyms: finish, stop)
2. *n* beginning
3. *vb* jump

state 1. *n* condition, circumstance, situation, status, stage, phase, grade
2. *n* territory, province, dominion, commonwealth, country, colony, zone
3. *vb* mention, say, tell

steal 1. *vb* rob, swipe, snatch, shoplift, purloin, embezzle, burglarize, rifle, poach, pinch, pilfer, pocket, plagiarize, pirate, filch, take, seize, pillage
2. *vb* sneak
3. *n* bargain

stereotype 1. *n* convention, generalization, categorization, characterization, cliché
2. *vb* categorize, pigeonhole, characterize, label, generalize

stick 1. *vb* poke, jab, probe, stab, plunge, pierce, prick, spear, puncture, lance, gore, peck, penetrate, perforate, riddle, hit
2. *vb* adhere, cohere, glue, paste, tape, cling, cleave, join
3. *n* branch, limb, twig, stem, stalk, staff, stave, wand, cane, club, baton, bar, bat

stop 1. *vb* halt, pause, cease, terminate, brake, arrest, check, stem, discontinue, lift, finish (antonym: start)
2. *vb* prevent, bar
3. *vb* close

storm 1. *n* tempest, gale, rainstorm, snowstorm, blizzard, hailstorm, ice storm, hurricane, typhoon, cyclone, monsoon, tornado, nor'easter, squall, rain, wind, snow
2. *n* flood
3. *vb* attack
4. *vb* hurry

story 1. *n* narrative, account, history, saga, chronicle, tale, narration, anecdote, yarn, plot, scenario, version, report, myth, joke, description
2. *n* lie
3. *n* floor

straight 1. *adj* direct, undeviating, even, unbent, regular, linear, true, level, vertical (antonyms: bent, zigzag)
2. *adj* sincere

strange 1. *adj* unfamiliar, unusual, unknown, unaccustomed, outlandish, foreign, new (antonym: common)
2. *adj* odd, peculiar, curious, abnormal, eccentric, quaint, queer, weird, eerie, bizarre, unnatural, ludicrous, different, irregular, mysterious, funny

strengthen 1. *vb* intensify, magnify, amplify, increase, expand, enhance, enlarge, boost, augment, swell, grow
2. *vb* fortify, brace, buttress, reinforce, harden, support

stress 1. *n* pressure, tension, strain, duress, worry
2. *n* accent
3. *vb* emphasize

strong 1. *adj* powerful, mighty, almighty, hardy, stalwart, robust, muscular, vigorous, athletic, virile, burly, tough, invincible, healthy (antonym: weak)
2. *adj* solid, sturdy, durable, sound, substantial, tough
3. *adj* potent, powerful, formidable, violent, forceful, intense
4. *adj* smelly

structure 1. *n* composition, arrangement, shape, form, pattern
2. *n* building
3. *vb* arrange

stubborn *adj* obstinate, headstrong, pertinaceous, dogged, opinionated, obdurate, tenacious, pigheaded, unrelenting, unruly, intractable, difficult, perverse, unmanageable, mulish, ornery, resolute, dogmatic, wild

student *n* pupil, learner, scholar, disciple, schoolchild, schoolgirl, schoolboy, freshman, sophomore, junior, senior, undergraduate, trainee, apprentice

study 1. *vb* analyze, evaluate, think through, pore over, review, research, criticize, survey, poll, canvass, examine, consider, learn, read
2. *n* examination, analysis, investigation, inquiry, exploration, survey, poll, census, sampling, probe
3. *n* report
4. *n* den
5. *n* dream

stupid *adj* ignorant, unintelligent, vacuous, foolish, dull, thoughtless (antonym: smart)

subject 1. *n* theme, topic, question, substance, matter, thesis, gist, point, text, issue, field
2. *n* course
3. *n* model, patient
4. *n* citizen
5. *vb* control

subtract *vb* deduct, remove, withhold, diminish, decrease (antonym: add)

success *n* accomplishment, achievement, attainment, progress, prosperity, victory, luck

sudden *adj* immediate, abrupt, swift, meteoric, precipitate, instantaneous, unexpected, unforeseen, sharp, early

suggest 1. *vb* recommend, urge, propose, advise, counsel, move, submit, prescribe, offer
2. *vb* imply, hint, intimate, insinuate

summary *n* outline, synopsis, abstract, paraphrase, condensation, abridgment, digest, précis, rundown, essence

supply 1. *n* stock, store, stockpile, inventory, reserve, hoard, cache, mine, holding, account, fund, reservoir
2. *vb* provide, equip, outfit, furnish, provision, rig, give, sell

support 1. *vb* bear, hold (up), bolster (up), brace, sustain, prop (up), buttress, carry, nourish, nurture, feed, promote, foster, strengthen
2. *vb* uphold, sustain, maintain, champion, enforce, back, help, approve
3. *vb* afford
4. *n* backing, encouragement, assistance, succor, maintenance, livelihood, subsistence, upkeep, resource, help, protection, approval, permission, incentive,

pension (antonym: opposition)
5. *n* mainstay, pillar, backer, champion, patron, fan
6. *n* brace, prop, buttress, stay, bolster, truss, reinforcement, base, basis

surprise 1. *vb* startle, amaze, astonish, daze, dazzle, bedazzle, flabbergast, throw, floor, shock
2. *n* amazement, astonishment, wonder, incredulity, shock
3. *n* gift

surrender 1. *vb* yield, concede, submit, resign, relinquish, sacrifice, acquiesce, capitulate, quit, give (in), bow, accede, defer, succumb, relent, lose, abandon
2. *n* submission, capitulation, resignation, acquiescence, concession, abdication, renunciation, forfeit, sacrifice

suspicious 1. *adj* distrustful, wary, leery, paranoid, apprehensive, jealous
2. *adj* suspect, queer, shady, dubious, doubtful, strange

swing 1. *vb* sway, rock, oscillate, vibrate, fluctuate, undulate, wave, roll, wobble, pitch, lurch, reel, waddle, turn
2. *vb* wave, brandish, flourish, wield, whirl, twirl
3. *vb* hang
4. *n* rhythm, music

T

tact *n* judgment, poise, diplomacy, savoir faire, discretion, delicacy, circumspection, finesse

take 1. *vb* convey, deliver, transport, carry, bring, lead
2. *vb* get, receive
3. *vb* confiscate, appropriate, expropriate, commandeer, usurp, gain, seize, catch
4. *vb* ingest, swallow, eat, drink
5. *vb* bear
6. *vb* choose
7. *vb* take in, earn

talent *n* gift, aptitude, genius, skill, expertise, flair, knack, prowess, adroitness, facility, ability, agility, specialty, art

talk 1. *vb* speak, converse, discuss, chat, communicate, confer, consult, parley, rap, argue, chatter, say, tell
2. *n* conversation, discussion, dialogue, consultation, word, chat, chitchat, patter, prattle, gibberish, speech, rumor, meeting

tax 1. *n* duty, tariff, toll, levy, fee, assessment, tribute
2. *vb* tire

teach *vb* instruct, educate, train, school, tutor, coach, lecture, inform, drill, enlighten, explain, preach

team 1. *n* squad, company, unit, crew, side, group
2. *n* (in reference to horses, mules, or oxen) pair, span, yoke, string, tandem

tell *vb* report, narrate, relate, recite, declare, inform, announce, disclose, communicate, convey, notify, state, profess, pronounce, tattle, say, talk, order, warn, testify, predict

temporary *adj* transitory, fleeting, momentary, ephemeral, provisional, stopgap, makeshift, interim, acting, short (antonym: permanent)

term 1. *n* word

2. *n* semester, trimester, quarter, tenure, period

3. *n* qualification, limitation, condition, restriction, stipulation, reservation, clause

theory *n* hypothesis, conjecture, speculation, supposition, premise, presumption, assumption, surmise, idea, reason, philosophy

therefore *adv* consequently, hence, accordingly, thus, ergo, wherefore, for, so

thick 1. *adj* dense, compact, close, condensed, packed, impenetrable, profuse (antonym: thin)

2. *adj* stiff, firm, viscous, syrupy, gelatinous, glutinous, viscid

3. *adj* broad

thin 1. *adj* flimsy, slim, slender, sheer, delicate, diaphanous, insubstantial, gossamer, weak (antonyms: thick, heavy)

2. *adj* narrow

3. *adj* slender, slim, lean, slight, skinny, scrawny, lanky, lank, wiry, spare, gaunt, haggard, emaciated (antonyms: big, tough)

4. *vb* weaken, disappear

think 1. *vb* reason, deliberate, cogitate, consider, meditate, believe

2. *vb* guess

thoughtful 1. *adj* considerate, sympathetic, tactful, solicitous, sensitive, friendly, polite, kind, nice (antonym: thoughtless)

2. *adj* meditative, contemplative, pensive, reflective, wistful, sad, absorbed, intellectual

thoughtless *adj* inconsiderate, careless, reckless, wanton, heedless, rash, foolhardy, ungrateful, thankless, unappreciative, rude, abrupt, indiscriminate, negligent (antonym: thoughtful)

throw 1. *vb* pitch, toss, hurl, fling, cast, pass, heave, chuck, sling

2. *vb* project, propel, launch, catapult, emit, radiate, send, give off, shoot

3. *vb* confuse, surprise

4. *vb* defeat

5. *n* toss, pitch, pass, cast

ticket 1. *n* pass, admission, voucher, permit, visa, passport, receipt, sales slip, slip

2. *n* ballot

3. *n, vb* label

tie 1. *vb* fasten, secure, knot, bind, lash, tether, hitch, lace, strap, join, link

2. *n* necktie, bow tie, cravat, ascot

3. *n* draw, deadlock, stalemate, standoff

tired 1. *adj* exhausted, weary, worn out, sleepy, fatigued, listless, drained, dead

2. *adj* trite

together 1. *adv* jointly, mutually, collectively, en masse, cooperatively (antonym: apart)
2. *adv* simultaneously, concurrently, contemporaneously

tool 1. *n* instrument, utensil, machine, appliance, gadget, implement, device, mechanism, apparatus, means, vehicle, medium, equipment, hammer
2. *n* instrument, pawn, puppet, stooge, dupe, victim

top 1. *n* peak, summit, pinnacle, apex, apogee, zenith, crest, tip, surface, climax, acme, prime, ultimate (antonym: base)
2. *n* cover, lid, cap, hood, stopper, cork, plug, bung
3. *adj* best
4. *vb* defeat, exceed

total 1. *n* sum, whole, aggregate, amount, totality, entirety, all (antonym: part)
2. *adj* all, complete
3. *vb* add

touch 1. *vb* feel, handle, caress, manipulate, paw, clutch, grope, rub
2. *vb* contact, meet, reach, border
3. *vb* concern
4. *n* feeling, sense
5. *n* bit

tough 1. *adj* sturdy, durable, stout, unbreakable, rugged, resilient, firm, strong
2. *adj* hard
3. *n* bully, vandal

town *n* city, village, municipality, township, hamlet, community, borough, suburb, metropolis, megalopolis, settlement, neighborhood

trade 1. *vb* exchange, swap, barter, switch, substitute, interchange, traffic, trade in, sell, change
2. *n* exchange, swap, switch, substitution, sale
3. *n* business, profession

translate *vb* convert, interpret, decipher, decode, paraphrase, render, transcribe, transliterate, paraphrase, transform

trash *n* garbage, rubbish, refuse, waste, debris, litter, rubble, flotsam, wreckage, junk

travel 1. *vb* journey, voyage, tour, cruise, trek, commute, explore, traverse, roam, visit, sail, go, wander
2. *n* passage, transportation, traffic, transit, trip

trick 1. *n* stunt, illusion, hoax, artifice, ploy, ruse, device, stratagem, deception, subterfuge, wile, dodge, joke, trap, pretense
2. *vb* cheat, betray

trip 1. *n* journey, voyage, tour, excursion, expedition, cruise, passage, drive, travel, jaunt, outing, spin, pilgrimage, odyssey
2. *vb* stumble, slip, lurch, sprawl, fall
3. *vb* dance

trivial *adj* petty, trifling, unimportant, negligible, frivolous, paltry, piddling, insignificant, meager, small, minute, minor, mere, superficial

trouble 1. *n* difficulty, predicament, plight, problem, matter, quandary, fix, pinch, strait, pickle, jam, spot, ordeal, mischief, hardship, nuisance
2. *vb* inconvenience, distress, afflict, ail, harry, bother, disturb, worry

truth 1. *n* truthfulness, verity, authenticity, veracity, candor, sincerity, openness, accuracy, honesty, certainty (antonym: lie)
2. *n* certainty

try 1. *vb* attempt, strive, struggle, essay, endeavor, venture, undertake, tackle, take on
2. *vb* test, sample, check, taste, experiment
3. *vb* prosecute, sue, indict, adjudicate, impeach, arraign, blame
4. *n* attempt, bid, endeavor, go, effort, trial, shot, stab, whirl

turn 1. *vb* spin, revolve, rotate, twirl, swirl, whirl, wheel, swivel, pivot, gyrate, wind, coil, hinge, flip, bend, swing, swerve
2. *n* curve, corner, round

type 1. *n* kind, sort, class, nature, manner, style, category, species, variety, race, breed, strain, genre, make
2. *n* print

U

ugly *adj* unsightly, repulsive,

hideous, grotesque, loathsome, revolting, repellent, repugnant, horrid, grisly, plain (antonym: pretty)

unaware *adj* ignorant, oblivious, obtuse, unmindful, unconscious, unconcerned, blind, deaf, heedless, naïve

unbelievable *adj* incredible, unimaginable, implausible, improbable, indescribable, unlikely, impossible, doubtful

uncomfortable *adj* ill at ease, discomfited, cramped, painful, distressful, disagreeable, agonizing, anxious, nervous (antonym: comfortable)

under 1. *prep* below, beneath, underneath (antonym: above)
2. *prep* less than, lower than, inferior to, subject to, subordinate to

unfaithful *adj* false, traitorous, treacherous, disloyal, perfidious, false-hearted, fickle, dishonest (antonym: faithful)

unfortunate *adj* unlucky, unhappy, hapless, disastrous, catastrophic, tragic, adverse, regrettable, lamentable, deplorable, sad, poor, pitiful

union 1. *n* unification, fusion, amalgamation, coupling, confluence, combination, marriage, merger, consolidation, link, wedding
2. *n* association, alliance, federation, league, partnership, guild, organization

unique *adj* unprecedented, incomparable, singular, peerless, unparalleled, unrivaled, unsurpassed, matchless, idiosyncratic, different, special, only

unnecessary *adj* needless, unessential, irrelevant, extraneous, superfluous, redundant, optional, gratuitous, pointless, extra, surplus, leftover, useless, excessive

unprepared *adj* unready, unsuspecting, inexperienced, napping, unwary

unreliable 1. *adj* (used in reference to persons) untrustworthy, irresponsible, fickle, undependable, unfaithful, dishonest (antonym: reliable)
2. *adj* (used in reference to ideas and inanimate objects or things) deceptive, unsound, misleading, flimsy, wrong

upset 1. *vb* overturn, capsize, topple, upend, invert, tip
2. *vb, n* defeat
3. *vb* worry, disturb, anger
4. *adj* angry
5. *n* shock

urban *adj* city, metropolitan, municipal, civic, cosmopolitan

urgent *adj* crucial, pressing, imperative, compelling, desperate, dire, acute, important

use 1. *vb* employ, utilize, wield, practice, exercise, exert, apply, expend, exploit, refer to, resort to, operate
2. *vb* consume, deplete, exhaust, expend, finish
3. *n* application, utilization, utility, usefulness, usage, purpose, operation, employment, consumption, expenditure, exercise, function, worth

useful *adj* helpful, practical, handy, beneficial, desirable, advantageous, profitable, pragmatic, utilitarian, versatile, efficient (antonym: useless)

useless 1. *adj* futile, vain, fruitless, unavailing, hopeless, desperate, abortive, unsuccessful, ineffectual, unprofitable, unnecessary (antonym: useful)
2. *adj* worthless, unusable, ineffective, counterproductive, broken

usual *adj* regular, customary, accustomed, habitual, ordinary, normal, set

V

vacation *n* holiday, recess, leave, furlough, sabbatical, respite, rest, R & R, break, leisure

valuable *adj* precious, dear, cherished, prized, beloved, inestimable, important, worthwhile, priceless, expensive, rare

variable *adj* changeable, unsettled, mutable, erratic, uncertain, uneven, inconsistent, arbitrary, fickle, unsteady

verify *vb* determine, prove, confirm, ascertain, ensure, assure, show, demonstrate, establish, authenticate, corroborate, substantiate, vindicate, defend, decide

very *adv* extremely, unusually, greatly, absolutely, immensely, terribly, awfully, rather, really, quite, most, too, much

victory *n* triumph, conquest, subjugation, mastery, overthrow, ascendancy, win (antonym: defeat)

view 1. *n* sight, glimpse, scene, scenery, vision, panorama, outlook, spectacle, perspective, prospect, vista, look
2. *n* belief
3. *vb* look, study
4. *vb* believe

violent 1. *adj* savage, fierce, furious, fuming, enraged, berserk, angry, belligerent, mean, wild, destructive
2. *adj* strong, stormy

virtue 1. *n* integrity, morality, honor, trustworthiness, principle, decency, goodness, truth, honesty, kindness
2. *n* innocence, purity, modesty, chastity, virginity
3. *n* advantage, worth

visible *adj* observable, discernible, perceptible, perceivable, visual, optical, graphic, illustrative, obvious

visit 1. *vb* call on/upon, stay with, drop by/in, sojourn, frequent, travel
2. *n* call, stay, appointment, sojourn, visitation, get-together

voluntary *adj* intentional, deliberate, willful, willing, freely, spontaneous, optional

vote 1. *n* ballot, election, referendum, poll, polls, tally, choice
2. *vb* choose, decide

vulnerable *adj* defenseless, unarmed, unprotected, unguarded, susceptible, prone, disposed, weak

W

wage *n* salary, pay, allowance, fee, tip, compensation, income, earnings, profit, intake, stipend, revenue, return, pension

wait *vb* remain, linger, loiter, stay, tarry, await, abide, dally, delay, hesitate (antonym: leave)

walk 1. *vb* amble, stroll, march, step, hike, stride, trudge, plod, lumber, file, trek, traipse, tramp, wander, strut, crawl
2. *n* gait
3. *n* path

want 1. *vb* wish, desire, crave, yearn, long, pine, hanker, itch, envy, hope, prefer
2. *vb* need
3. *n* lack, dearth, paucity, shortage, scarcity, deficiency, absence, hardship, poverty

warn *vb* forewarn, caution, alert, tip off, advise, admonish, exhort, counsel, scare, tell

waste 1. *vb* squander, fritter away, dissipate, misuse, misspend (antonym: save)

2. *vb* decrease

3. *n* trash

4. *n* desert

5. *adj* sterile

wave 1. *n* billow, swell, surge, tidal wave, ripple, breaker, roller, whitecap, comber, surf

2. *vb* motion, gesture, signal, beckon, flag, salute

3. *vb* flutter, flap, ripple, sway, blow, swing

weak *adj* frail, feeble, infirm, invalid, helpless, powerless, unfit, impotent, puny, delicate, fragile, flimsy, rickety, breakable, thin, sick, vulnerable (antonym: strong)

wealth *n* riches, affluence, means, opulence, luxury, prosperity, assets, fortune, treasure, hoard, money, property, abundance

weather 1. *n* climate, conditions, clime

2. *vb* age, season, wear, endure, harden

3. *vb* expose, overcome, bear

weight 1. *n* heaviness, heft, mass, substance, pressure, load, density, measure

2. *n* importance

welcome 1. *vb* greet, receive, salute, address, herald, hail, call, entertain, appreciate

2. *n* greeting, salutation, reception

3. *n* hospitality

well 1. *adv* properly, thoroughly, competently, satisfactorily, adequately, excellently, splendidly

2. *adv* favorably, kindly, approvingly, highly

3. *adj* healthy

4. *n* spring, reservoir, cistern, fountain, source

5. *n* shaft, bore, hole

wet 1. *adj* soaked, drenched, saturated, sodden, soggy, dripping, damp, liquid (antonym: dry)

2. *adj* rainy, drizzly, stormy, inclement, misty, showery, snowy, slushy

3. *vb* moisten, soak, dampen, sprinkle, saturate, drench, douse, water, steep, immerse, rinse

white *adj* ivory, milky, snowy, silvery, snow-white, frosty, creamy, fair, pale (antonym: black)

wild 1. *adj* untamed, fierce, ferocious, savage, raging, turbulent, fiery, violent, mean, rough, stormy

2. *adj* uncultivated, overgrown, rampant, overrun

3. *adj* disorderly, unruly, obstinate, undisciplined, stubborn

4. *n* country

will 1. *n* willpower, determination, resolution, volition, conviction, resolve, willfulness, ambition

2. *n* testament, bequest, inheritance

3. *vb* leave

win 1. *vb* triumph, prevail, succeed, overcome, defeat (antonym: lose)

2. *vb* score, achieve, earn, get

3. *n* victory

wisdom *n* judgment, reason, understanding, appreciation, intelligence, intellect, comprehension, sagacity, perception, discernment, sense, common sense, knowledge, experience, depth

word 1. *n* term, expression, locution, utterance, vocable, verbalism, articulation, syllable
2. *n* talk
3. *n* promise

work 1. *n* labor, toil, effort, drudgery, exertion, industry, endeavor, pains, travail
2. *n* job, profession
3. *n* accomplishment, undertaking, composition, creation, opus, act, book, picture, poem
4. *vb* toil, labor, strive, struggle, slave, strain, act, do
5. *vb* work out, solve

worry 1. *n* concern, care, anxiety, apprehension, burden, fear
2. *vb* upset, concern, trouble, fret, brood, stew, disturb, bother

worst *adj* meanest, lowest, bad, least (antonym: best)

worth *n* value, benefit, merit, virtue, estimation, importance, price, use

wrap 1. *vb* gift wrap, cover, bind, envelop, shroud, clothe, swathe, sheathe, swaddle, bandage
2. *n* shawl, muffler, cloak, cape, mantle, stole, scarf

write 1. *vb* inscribe, jot, record, scribble, scrawl, transcribe, sign
2. *vb* compose, draft, indite, pen, author, publish, edit, compile, print

wrong 1. *adj* incorrect, false, mistaken, inaccurate, untrue, erroneous, invalid, bad, corrupt, amiss, awry, improper, illogical, immoral (antonyms: correct, right)
2. *n* crime

X ray 1. *n* radiation, ultraviolet ray, gamma ray
2. *n* radiograph, encephalogram, photograph

yell *vb, n* call, shout, scream, shriek, screech, bellow, thunder, rant, rave, harangue, boo, hiss, jeer, hoot, squall, cry

yes *interj* aye, okay, OK, affirmative, amen, certainly (antonym: no)

young *adj* youthful, immature, juvenile, adolescent, boyish, girlish, underage, childish, new (antonym: old)

Z

zero *n* nothing, naught, nought, none, nil, love (in tennis), cipher

zone 1. *n* area, region, district, belt, band, quarter, place
2. *vb* divide